THE MYSTERY PUZZLE OF LOVE

Life Of Valuable Energy

Pam Halbert

National Library of Australia Cataloguing-in-Publication entry

A catalogue record for this book is available from the National Library of Australia

NATIONAL LIBRARY OF AUSTRALIA

978-0-9943834-8-8 (paperback)

978-0-9943834-9-5 (hardback)

978-0-6488317-0-9 (eBook)

Publishing Consultants.

Cover and interior layout: Pickawoowoo Publishing Group

Cover Art: Jill Fryer

Publisher.

Pam Halbert, Western Australia. For permission requests and quantity order discounts please contact the publisher by email at: cphalbert@bigpond.com

Printing.

Lightning Source (USA, UK, AUS, EUR).

Contents

THE PREFACE

This Book is not Fiction it is real life, it is my voice, my values and persuasion from my own and many other people bad experiences and can prevent it happening to you. It is my voice and my values with my learning from listening, reading and studying over 60 years, and how my growth into happiness came through pain and suffering into healing and a truly free Spirit is possible and attainable. The book is to help and inform women and men how to find the pieces to their own human puzzle. Why we make mistakes and how we can prevent mistakes from becoming permanent pain and suffering. This is sometimes inflicted on us by others when we do not deserve abusive or bad treatment.

The following are 38 ACRONYMS I use throughout the book to give further meaning and understanding to the language we humans use. These words are Love, Freedom, Fear, Evil, Eternal, Grace, Life, Religion, Peace, Energy, Faith, Prayer, Holy Spirit, Wisdom, God, Creating, Gentle, Strength, Value, Aware,

Blame, Share, Trust, Discipline, Mind, Soul, Revenge, Judge, Justice, Anger, Inspire Truth, Hope Like, Confidence, Courage, Communication Acronym.

Where I use these words I apply the following meanings. This is to make us aware and to highlight our conscious and sub-conscious thoughts. Many people are not in touch with their sub-conscious thoughts or sometimes hide them. These can often be pain or suffering received in childhood, unintentionally or totally unaware how our early years develop our potential personality and character or may damage it and possibly cause mental disorders in Life. How we raise our children from the cradle through their young years and teens is the main foundation for their lives this becomes the basis to give them confidence, courage resilience to learn their own skills and free choices. This book is to encourage all men and women who are to become parents to find how the first 20 years of life are to build confidence for children to grow and learn their life is valuable with purpose, to become well balanced creative communicators with commitment and gentle strength for a healthy meaningful life from birth. To prevent domestic violence and suicide and be good citizens for themselves and the world and to cope with what life throws at them in their adult years as it is very difficult if neglected. After age 20 it is often too late because it is too hard to re-learn the lost 20 years when entering the School of Life. We humans have to know our own true value to be able to accept the true value of anyone else.

L.O.V.E. for me means LIFE OF VALUABLE ENERGY

Love is not a feeling, as feelings change three or four times a day depending on our experience. I believe Love is a decision made by men and women with our Will. For me Love is a Gift given to us at our birth by God is a "Life Of Valuable Energy". This Love God gifts us at our Birth is not a feeling but a desire made with God's Will and our Will. This Love is precious and should be treated with care, compassion kindness and valued by our parents or guardians. When we are nurtured and raised this way to our adult years, we should then be able to know HOW to make our own decisions. Not forced into WHAT someone else wants us to do. Yes we should listen for guidance with care and imagination then use our valuable energy to put our decision into action with joy, compassion, kindness and gentleness with positive attitudes and choices.. This involves our 3 Brains being balanced which I refer to later in the book. So we continue to progress in the world with joy, compassion, kindness, gentleness and all the positive feelings of security with our valuable energy. I hope with support from your family.

The following ACRONYMS for me mean.

A.W.A.R.E. - Awake with a Revelation Experience.

B.L.A.M.E. - Blind Life and Mind Energy.

G.E.N.T.L.E. - Good Essential News Tender Living Energy.

S.T.R.E.N.G.T.H. - Spiritual Trust Requires Early New Growth Then Health.

S.H.A.R.E. - Surrender Heart and Relational Experiences.

T.R.U.S.T. - Truthful Response Under Spiritual Tender

D.I.S.C.I.P.L.I.N.E. - Doing Inner Searching Courage In Personal Life's Internal Necessary Energy.

M.I.N.D. - Memory In Neutral Discipline.

S.O.U.L. - Spirit Of Understanding Love.

R.E.V.E.N.G.E. - Returned Evil Violence Enables Negative Growth Eternally.

J.U.D.G.E. - Justice Under Discipline Grows Eternally.

J.U.S.T.I.C.E. - Judged Under Strict Truth In Court Edit.

A.N.G.E.R. - A Negative Guarded Energy Response.

I.N.S.P.I.R.E. - Informing New Spiritual Prayer Is Responsible Energy.

V.A.L.U.E. - Vision Aware Love Understands Empathy

C.O.N.F.I.D.E.N.C.E. - Care of Newly Found Identity Driving Encourage New Creative Energy.

C.O.U.R.A.G.E. - Contains Order Under Real Adversity Great Effort

T.R.U.T.H. - Telling Reality Under Trouble Hearing.

H.O.P.E. - Helping Other People Eternally.

L.I.K.E. - Life in Kind Empathy.

C.O.M.M.U.N.I.C.A.T.I.O.N. - Conversing Our Memorable Moments Under Notice in Confident Action to Inform Our News.

F.R.E.E.D.O.M. - For Responsible Energy Enables Discipline Of Mind.

Freedom is not to do what we want to do, but to do what we ought to do, to balance a healthy, happy gentle strength to have courage to be creative when life throws sad and difficult events at us. Freedom is also a gift from God, because God does not make our choices. God is available for guidance and help when we trust Him and ask. This free Gift from God at our birth is firstly to choose God then our neighbour as our self, for a happy, healthy well balanced gentle strength to have courage to be creative when life throws sad or difficult events at us. It is not freedom to abuse or kill.

F.E.A.R. - Feelings Envy Anger Revenge.

These are negative feelings we may encounter as children in our early years, among others of pain, rejection, insecurity, abandonment or had our autonomy [choices or will] taken from us even if disabled. Fear, when irrational or unrealistic, can be self-destructive as well as harmful to others. All negative attitudes and selfish demands and lack of forgiveness destroy our heart, mind, self-control and give feelings of abandonment. These are not helpful attributes for raising children to have confidence and courage, creativity, communication and commitment to bring up these fearful feelings from the cradle through to their teens, and society has been seeing and hearing the results.

E.V.I.L. - Energy Violent In Life.

Evil comes from the root word Fear and is destructive to the valuable life energy of others, as well as family and friends of the perpetrator. This can include Global Nations and all creatures great and small. I believe we are being evil to our self when we deceive or are lying to our self and then pass it on to others. The word darkness is a metaphor for evil.

E.T.E.R.N.A.L. - Experience True Effort Reality Natural And Learned

For me Truth is Reality. When we see reality we can cope with making more advanced courses of action. Our road to reality is not easy. It is helpful to have a map of where we are in life and where we want to go. This takes effort to make accurate maps to appreciate, explore and recognize reality in our changing world of Eternal life. I believe Eternal Life begins at our birth and continues into the Kingdom of God, when we trust God and use our gift of Life of Valuable Energy and choice of disciplined Freedom for God's purposes in Creation. Eternal Life is not earned it is the Trinity of Love, Freedom and Grace God's gifts to us.

G.R.A.C.E. - Gods Reasons And Christs Ethics.

Love [Life of Valuable Energy] is Conscious but Grace is not conscious the process of Grace means the only way to understand it is to accept this powerful force is outside our human conscious which nurtures our Spiritual growth. Without any proof my own personal view of Grace is the feminine attribute of God's nature and exists as a paradox which is real within God's nature and character. This is often referred to as a doctrine of Immanence, which says that Grace comes out from God within the centre of human Beings. I believe God's Holy Spirit is male and female. When we acknowledge we are made in the Image of God and understand both the male and female attributes in our human nature, we can believe God's Holy Spirit is within us. God's Blessing to humans when they truly discover the Divine Gift and learn to follow Jesus as they journey towards God. Resistance to Grace is often when we are unaware of its Presence because we fail to appreciate the value of the gift when it is given.

L.I.F.E. - Living In Faithful Eternity

In John 20:31 we discover that Jesus is the Way the Truth and the Life. How we are to live this life can lead us to many adventurous and some painful hurdles to jump. We learn very young that life is not going to be easy, but with compassionate guidance it can also be delightful. In the Gospels the meaning of the word "Life" is not only about physical existence but also about identity. Matt 23:12 "who ever exalts him/her self shall be humbled and whoever humbles him/her self shall be exalted." This means to have confidence in our own skills and abilities, not with superiority but with confidence to listen to others. When Love [life of valuable energy] and Life [living in faithful eternity] become connected our true identity does what it truly wants to do and consequently loves whatever it does. Then every aspect of our life is changed, transformed 1Cor.15: 52-54 tells us. I believe Life energy was created out of chaos Genesis Chapters 1 and 2. can help us understand Hope was implanted in Creation from the beginning, so the great Mystery includes everything, nothing is wasted. Life is a God Created Mystery puzzle and I am exploring the meaning of Life with purpose.

R.E.L.I.G.I.O.N. - Responsible Energy Living In God's Image Of Need

A healthy religion should be an open and inclusive belief system with a trustworthy and disciplined community service to the people, as they search for their desired truth. All Spiritual teachers are to be helping people to find forgiveness for themselves and others as Jesus showed in Matthew 9:6 "get up, pick up your mat and go home". This was to help them and us to understand how all healing comes with confidence and courage in physical and mental relationships with a change in our attitudes and Faith in God's truth demonstrated in Jesus. This is to show that truth and goodness does not just educate us, it transforms us. This also reminds us that love not death is Eternal Life, and leads us to who we really are; love always wins. In the order of experience of self-discovery and God's knowledge is how we know anything, as Paul tells us in 1Cor.13:12 "then we shall know as fully as we are known", and we have nothing to be afraid of as long as we do not start with or end with fear, anger or judgment. "on that day you will know that you are in me and I am in you" John 14:20, this is the core message, promise and goal of all Religion. Religion is not doing its job if it constantly reminds us of our unworthiness, our sinfulness or inadequacy before God's Greatness. This increases the gap between us and the "supreme majesty of God". This is the very gap that Jesus came to deny and close, we should hear in Matthew 23:13 and Paul warns us against Religion as mere laws or purity codes as against Jesus' teaching of alternative wisdom.

P.E.A.C.E. - People Enrich And Care Equally

Peace has economic, political as well as military issues, Micah 4:34 his vision with the absence of fear. In both International peace and domestic social values strengthen each other and is a Biblical and secular dream of the Spirit our Life of Valuable Energy in human nature. We are living in a semi-time of peace but with a greater burden of anxiety this places a strain on social and moral standards, and with no guarantee of a reasonable future many seize the immediate pleasures of the day. This brings out the contradictions that confuse the Christian peace of the future and the Love ethic of the New Testament. Peace is an important social goal as humans find the greatest relationships of harmony for life.

E.N.E.R.G.Y. - Eternal Necessary Ethics Rewards Growing Youth.

Energy is action in working, to be active with force, vigor, effective or powerful. We humans live between the Alpha and the Omega of Eternity {the Beginning and up to the End of Eternity}. One aspect we are failing to live is good ethics with our energy which for me means Eternal Necessary Ethics Rewards Growing Youth. My reason for my Acronym is to unwrap this word for a clearer understanding of the important loss of how we learn our Ethics. Energy is part of Emotion as E-Motion is energy in action. In this situation how we use our moral ethics.

F.A.I.T.H. - Forgiveness Asked In Truthful Hope

Faithfulness and obedience experience work for good through God. In Romans 8 Paul lists bad experiences and teaches God will direct us through the Holy Spirit, the "paraclete" the Comforter will teach us all we need to know. It is not magic God uses other Christians to teach us. I had to be taught how to be a Priest I had to be willing to learn. Sometimes negative experiences can also teach us, and God comforts us in our troubles so we can give comfort to others. The charge at Ordination is—we will not try to do this on our own. God will equip us to do His/Her will. If you ask how does one acquire faith? Or how do we know we have faith? I believe Faith is part of our Soul when we are born. I know many people do not accept or recognize their own faith. They say they do not believe in God or that religious stuff, possibly influenced by parents. I believe God sent Jesus to teach us how to live a kind, compassionate and honest life with His teaching, parables and metaphors, a couple examples of metaphors:

1. The word HOME is used for our Soul.

2. The word SHEEP Jesus uses for people. John 10:16

3. Jesus is a metaphor for all Creation.

4. Darkness is a metaphor for evil.

5. Jesus uses other metaphors such as light, bride, salt, branch clay soil dove to help us have a better understanding that we are precious and valuable part of His Creation and called to live creatively, with gentle strength in a balanced state.

P.R.A.Y.E.R. - Praise Rendered After Your Effort Received.

To pray for true understanding for the coming of God's Kingdom is through Christ. The Lord's Prayer is universal not only

Jewish but for men and women of every age and race. Prayer must be an act of personal communion with God, which requires mental concentration and the shutting out of distractions Matthew 6:6 and Mark 1:35. Then the need for faith is stressed in Mark 11:24 and Luke 17:6 and the answer will come in John 15:7/16 when the prayer is in the Spirit of Christ and thus in line with God's Will 1John 5:14. Paul says in Romans 8:26 ff the prayers of the Prophets had special power because they were Spirit filled men. Now all Christians have the same Spirit so may pray with the same power. This indwelling Spirit we call the Holy Spirit is distinct from mans spirit. Some people find it difficult in shaping prayer and we need to understand that the Holy Spirit knows not only our mind but also the mind of God and therefore is able to frame our prayers with the Divine purpose.

H.O.L.Y. - Honour Our Lord Yearning.

When the Holy Spirit is operating in us we are the salt of the earth, Jesus used the metaphor "salt" for our Life of Valuable Energy [Love]

S.P.I.R.I.T. - Silent Prayer Is Revelation In Trust.

Some important meanings of Spirit are the Hebrew word "Ruach" and Greek word "Pneunia" mean Wind both destructive and gentle and in the Old Testament mainly depict wind as an instrument of the unseen God. Then "Breath" the air all Creation breathes is a "Spirit" of God's creative activity. The word Soul for the Hebrews was "man on earth" as well as a creature of God Isaiah 31:3. In Genesis 2:7 –6:17 –7:15 they have Spiritual characteristics of humility, depression even energy. The Spirit of God has a central place in the Christian message and at the heart of the message is Jesus anointed by the Spirit of God. Acts 4:26 and Luke 1:35 and John 1:32 and Romans 1:1-4. The story had great consequences as God ensured the Forgiveness of sins and men were called to repent. The Spirit was given to those who did repent and equipped for the task of spreading the Gospel message. Acts 2:38 with a mystical sense are metaphors wind, fire, descending doves, and flowing water are often used to describe the Holy Spirit.

W.I.S.D.O.M. - When I Secure Discipline Of Mind

Mainly found in the Old Testament in Job and Proverbs. Often refers to common sense, and sometimes trying to find the meaning of Life in difficult experiences. We can only know something when we can use it with deep wisdom and insight. The meaning of wisdom is linked with folly in the Bible Mathew 25:2 and Romans 1:22, these passages are developed by Paul in relation to God and Christ 1Corinthians 1:24,30 and Colossians 1:15-18. The wisdom of God is seen in what Christ did and who he was Mark 6:2. Thus Proverbs 8:22-31 suggests that wisdom was pre-existent before Creation and since then mankind. Paul emphasizes the uniqueness of Christ and his thoughts are parallel to John and the word of God in Colossians 1. These passages are the full understanding that the Redeemer is the Creator of the Universe.

G.O.D. - Goodness Overcomes Death

Old Testament literature shows in the time of Deutero-Isaiah 538 B.C. years before Christ taught that Jahweh was the Creator of the world, Lord of all nature Director of History and the only God that we may know, believe and understand. This was further developed in Judaism with God's relationship with the Spirit and the Word and is considered the meaning that combines Eternal Reason with Eternal Revelation in the Gospel of John and identified with Christ. Jesus limited his missionary to Israel Matthew 15:24 He declared the Gospel should be preached to all nations. In John 10:15-16 Jesus uses the word "Sheep" as a metaphor for humans, that there are other sheep outside the fold of Judaism, and teaches that God is the Father of all humans not merely Christians and His love and mercy extends to even bad men or women for He lets His sun shine and rain fall on the just and the unjust Matthew 5:45. God is ready to forgive any sinner who repents as shown in His parable of the Prodical son in Luke 15.

C.R.E.A.T.I.N.G. - Courage Requires Effort And Trust In Nurturing Growth.

God is into Creation not feelings. God creates Nature, Birds, Animals, Humans and God creates through us with God's guided imagination as co-creators when we follow Him/Her.

The word ACRONYM for me means: A Creative Responsible Opinion Naming Your Meaning. You may find your own meanings to these words.

I use these Acronyms to help unpack a deeper meaning of these words we use, with more in the following chapters of how our language translations from Aramaic, to Hebrew to Greek to Latin and to English to name a few may change our understanding of words and cause confusion. It is well documented in the Bible and many other well educated and experienced authors in the various cultures and religions in our world. If we want inner peace and how to use our gift of valuable energy we have to start with our self. I am hoping to help women how to tackle their pain and suffering by opening the door to finding their own happiness by self assessment and honest self-discovery as no one else is going to do it for them. This can be from poor early training from the cradle which was taught in the young years and has to be relearned, because some parents are selfish and do not value their children. Or we may chose to ignore good advice and learning in our early years and turn it into bad habits and attitudes which we can correct. Then forgiveness of our self is the first and greatest healing we can do even if parents or guardians have died or are still alive.

"Mystery" occurs only in the New Testament in Paul's Epistles. The sense is different to our modern day use of the word. The modern usage may be defined as a secret or riddle to which an answer has not been found. In the New Testament "Mystery" is a Divine secret and remains a Mystery that does not become transparent to humans. In the Gospel of Mark 4:11 ff. it refers to the Kingdom of God. Paul uses the term to refer to God's purpose of salvation in the revelation of Jesus Christ. This is the revelation in EPH.6:19 and COL.2:2 which was hidden and now made known in Christ.

For Paul the Mystery relates to the inclusion of the Gentiles ROM. 16:26 and EPH.1:9 ff --- EPH.3:3-6 as well as the Jews COL. 1:27 and PHIL. 3:8. History says Paul borrowed the term "Mystery" from the ancient Greek speaking "word" the people used centuries before Christ.

I call the Mystery of Life a jigsaw journey to find the missing pieces we need for life is a God made mystery puzzle. Our attitudes and approach to our life should be one of self-care and value as a gift from God. This process of HOW, WHAT, WHEN, WHERE, WHY starts here with HOW well we were received at our birth, nurtured, trained and loved by our parents or guardians. So, that we develop, our unique identity and understand how to grow up our humanity. What happens growing up our physical body we may find challenging or exciting. We may find developing our mental capacities, difficult or energizing. When it comes to discovering our soul/ spirit [feelings and emotions] it requires a well informed, gentle and valued trust in God to dig deep into the core of our Being. Sadly many men and boys find it too hard and miss out on the peace, valued, true disciplined Freedom of the real meaning and purpose of living in this wonderful world that God has gifted to us. This is where we begin to discover our identity and develop a true self-assessment of HOW we want to live our life and the skills and abilities we will train and explore for the future.

We know how we arrived here through our parents, but we do not know where we have come from. The Mystery is WHY, WHAT, WHEN, WHERE AND HOW do we understand God's Gift of Life and the application to survive with Love not Fear. The Mystery Puzzle is a life journey that maybe short or long, fruitful or fearful, joyful or tearful, controlling or spiritual [meaning God's help the Holy Spirit].

WHAT is my message? I write to encourage to persuade with my life experience and those who I have had the privilege to touch and care for, studied and learned information a helpful and hopeful process to discover HOW the missing pieces of our life puzzle can be found. Then to learn WHERE to put the pieces into the puzzle and to open our heart and mind to HOW misinformation about

God can prevent us from seeking God's Kingdom. This means we need to unlearn some fearful language and teaching and to re-learn WHY and HOW God is a God of Love [Life of Valuable Energy] and not a God of Fear [Feelings Envy Anger Revenge].

Searching the BIBLE is the most meaningful, life giving, beautiful, joy filled puzzle we will explore and create in our life. We all need meaning to understand why we are alive and on earth. We are invited to be Co-Creators as partners with God in His\ Her Creation. Jesus is a metaphor for all Creation and Home is a metaphor for our Soul.

I do not tell people what to do to solve their problems. It is their freedom of choice. God does not make our choices for us. I like to follow Disraeli who said "the good you can do with your gifts and riches for others, is to show them their own gifts and riches." Sadly some people are too fearful to take the risks when they lack confidence.

I see all the opportunities that come my way as jigsaw puzzles. This particular one is the Holy Spirit calling me to take the risk of sharing my life struggles. Life is a jigsaw of experiences and only God knows how and when it will be completed. My Prayer and Hope are to help people find CHRIST who is within us. The Holy Spirit is available for us and that we are all a piece of the puzzle as co-creators with God. The Holy Spirit continues to renew the whole Creation and we see when we want to that with God nothing is impossible. Albert Einstein said 'the world we have created is a process of our thinking. It cannot be changed unless we change our thinking."

Shakespeare said—"There is no evil unless our thinking make it so."

So it seems to me the world we have created with our collective human thinking needs a serious overhaul. An awareness of HOW, WHAT, WHEN, WHERE AND WHY the chaos we are creating is the arrogance of human indulgence and self motivated greed by humans creating their own POWER. It is one thing to be satisfied with self-esteem when solving a man made puzzle. However a Life of

Valued Energy and God's gift of disciplined freedom should be THE CREATIVE guide to a GENTLE STRENGTH OF BALANCED SHARED POWER. Not the negative sub-conscious anger that many humans are using to destroy God's wonderful Creation, our World.

I pray this Book and Freedom Revisited my previous book will help guide our thinking for future generations from the Cradle. So, that there is "nothing as strong as gentleness and nothing as gentle as real strength" because when we put strength and gentleness together we get well balanced creative energy and power. To raise boys and girls with balanced thinking we all need to move from surviving by fear and anger to Love and Compassion for all people and creatures great and small. With God's Grace humanity needs this to THRIVE, not just survive.

This Mystery Puzzle exists between the ALPHA and OMEGA of ETERNAL LIFE.

May God Bless you from the Beginning to the End of your Life.

ACKNOWLEDGMENT

To my daughters Susie and Jules for their constant training and help using the Word Computer with their loving patience with me.

To Ian Jones I am most grateful for reading and giving literary, coherent and thoughtful suggestions.

To Jill Fryer a big thank you for her amazing artwork for the cover.

To Julie Ann Harper and the Pickawoowoo Publishing Group for their caring, professional encouragement and help with lots of paper hugs from me.

Chapter 1

LIFE ARRIVING AND GROWING

Genesis 1:27.

L.I.F.E. Living in Faithful Eternity

I arrived with a sharp shock as I was pulled from my comfortable womb, into a noisy gulping atmosphere, which I learnt some time later was my new place to live. The shock was a slap on my bottom I was told was to make me gulp some new air, that was God's breathe that I will need while I live in this new place. Then I let them know I was here to stay with a loud cry of distress, not one of eustress [euphobia] joy at my arrival into this new world, but one of control as this seemed to get their attention. I soon learned this became a future signal for further attention to fulfill my needs, as the automatic food supply seemed to close down. Then this became the best way of gaining their attention every time I did not feel comfortable. This was the beginning of growing my Body, which was to last over twenty years. A few months later I found I had a Mind I had to grow up as well. I will explain later how I had to make the connection to grow up my Spirit.

If we are not fortunate to have immediate care, even though we are born with God's LOVE, [this is—Life Of Valued Energy] Right now is to learn Love is not a feeling---it is a decision, our Will to make a Free Choice with the other Gift from God called FREEDOM.

We soon learn this Love is not to be taken for granted or even unconditional love may not be available. So we soon become aware of how our parents or guardians show their emotions when we want our needs met. This awareness can be negative and frightening when our activity increases and punishment is the response at a tender age.

There is an old saying, "a man/woman reaps what he/she sows". Sometimes depending on the attitude and understanding of the parent or guardian, disobedient treatment when very young can be brutal and cause fear which can cause permanent damage of physical and mental suffering. This negativity that comes from unhappy or unbalanced parents or guardians, adds to destructive forces that the very young take into their growing painful world. This evil or darkness in a person is an invasion of harmful impulses that come from purely human sources, even our sub-conscious mind, often gained from a traumatic youth, or unintentional misunderstanding from poor parenting.

All human beings are, BODY, MIND, SPIRIT. Fortunately our spiritual world in the whole human race contains good forces, with great Souls known to give love [valued energy] and protection to those who have been bewildered and disturbed with suffering. In the letter to the Hebrews 12:22-24, how God the Good Judge and the spirits of good men and women made perfect, will be their guardians in Heaven, MTT.18:10. The small children with spiritual sensitivity, and those who are ignored or rejected and more fearful of God, are closer to God and greater in acceptance. In the Old Testament the Sages of Israel taught "the fear of the Lord is the beginning of Wisdom" which may help the child's basic code of social behaviour. Sadly there is a much more cruel fear of unjust treatment by evil people on a helpless victim. This can be seen in our refugee camps and political greed in poor Countries. We first experience the fear of punishment when we are small helpless children. Their early identity is their small bodies in close contact with those who give them comfort, affection and warmth. Good discipline requires TIME. When we do not have Time for our children we are not able to observe them, to become aware of their special needs, and they are all different. If we are impatient or irritated we may impose the incorrect discipline of anger without checking the problem, or not take time to consider the most appropriate discipline. For me this is where" there is nothing as strong as gentleness and nothing as gentle as real strength" is the way to start to teach children how to solve problems without anger or violence, with gentle urging praise and thoughtful care.

Parents will observe how they play or study, when they run away from problems rather than face them, blame some one else rather than own up to their mistake. When parents are listening and watching their children, they can respond gently with adjustments of strength with little stories and hugs and kisses, or pats on the back for honest answers. Sometimes this can be a shared suffering with a child and the children are not blind to this. This helps children realize that suffering that is shared with Mum or Dad is not so bad and cope better. This is the beginning of self discipline. This quality time tells children they are valued by their parents. If only words of affection are used and no action, the children are not deceived by hollow words. They know their parents do not match up with deeds of value. The feeling of being valuable is essential for mental health and self discipline. It is a direct product of parental love such conviction must be gained in childhood. All children fear abandonment which begins at about six months, as soon as a child is able to perceive itself to be separate from its parents, and realizing it is totally helpless and dependent at the mercy of its parents for all forms of survival. Abandonment by parents, such as "Mummy and Daddy aren't going to forget about you," OR "Mummy and Daddy are not going to leave you behind". These words if matched by deeds year in and year out, by the time of their teens they will lose the fear of abandonment. Instead have a deep inner feeling that their world is a safe place.

Of course many are not so fortunate. Sadly some children are abandoned during their childhood by death, desertion or negligence, others fail to receive reassurance by poor parenting with threats to enforce discipline "if you don't do exactly as I want you to do I won't love you any more." That means death or abandonment,

3

which is using LOVE as a force of control and domination over their children. So these children enter adulthood perceiving the world as a frightening and dangerous place with little security for the future. This is painful and difficult to achieve as an adult, and is hard to destroy when they know they are valued and take care of themselves in all ways necessary, so self discipline becomes self caring. This also applies to their TIME they will want to share with their parents. These Gifts are the most precious GIFTS that any parent can give their children. It is possible to receive them from other sources, as I did when my Mother died when I was ten years old. This was an up hill struggle but worth the effort to enjoy our wonderful world.

As we humans grow and develop while learning to understand this new world we find ourselves. Some experience love, others limited or negligent treatment. Why do some have these bad experiences of the absence of care and compassion? If this is a continued way of being raised, it can become a reason behind poor mental health when older. However a few manage to wind their way through rough waters so to speak. Then some show a few are able to transcend their troubled childhood to become well balanced mature people. For me this is the Grace of God that we may be led into, outside the early unhelpful treatment, by Grandparents or teachers that enter our lives. Later in the book I endeavour to unfold some ideas how God's Grace saves us. These early discoveries of Life 0f Valuable Energy [Love] we receive at our birth from God.

I call this the beginning of The School of Life, where discipline becomes a lesson. Because we are learning so much so quickly, we understand at times we fail to achieve our desire. Depending on which culture and religion we are being raised, as to the ideas and beliefs that are formed and naturally developed. There are many different views of the world we are exploring and for most of our early years our mind and our emotions are not formed or completely conscious of the world view we are developing. If we do not start from the cradle, the very young years, the results are evident by the time they are 10 years old. This becomes very hard to change once early mistakes are made and unhelpful habits develop, when anger and punishment are used for control. What is said and done becomes a child's sub-conscious of how to treat people. We must all move away from threatening control and abuse. From Fear to Love and compassion if future generations are to have meaning and purpose in their lives and not just fear of how to survive.

When leaving school I was asked "what was the most valuable lesson I had learned to help me in Life." My answer was "I have learned how to educate myself for the remainder of my life. This is still relevant for me to-day. For me there needs to be meaning in Life so we have a purpose for learning even when it is challenging. We have thrown the baby out with the bath water of God's gifts of Love and Freedom, with our sometimes lazy and selfish thoughts and fear. We are teaching our children WHAT to think instead of HOW to think and find their own truth. So our thinking and mind games need a necessary overhaul. Life is a Valuable School in which we all have lessons to learn. I found this message over 60 years ago "there is nothing as strong as gentleness and nothing as gentle as real strength". I was taught at school when I asked why I was always made class Captain, my teacher told me I had gentle strength with my class mates. Gentleness is not a weakness, I believe it is a virtue of a well balanced man and father. I have sadly buried a number of young selfish angry controlling men [6 suicides]. Far too many of our present fathers are absent or training their sons to be fearful and angry, which speaks very loudly how they experienced their own upbringing. If men understood that strength comes through gentleness, kindness, their maleness would be more valuable to themselves and to society with confident communication. Parents of all ages need to be aware of how our boys are NOT being taught.

1. How to solve conflict without violence.

2. How to live without irrational fear.

3. How to love [life of valuable energy] without angry conditions, usually discovered after marriage with lack of communication.

If we do not move beyond our fear based preoccupations we will not improve our human and Spiritual development. Matt.16; 26 "what will profit you if you gain the whole world and lose your very Soul". There is too much offensive and defensive behaviour in our early years. This makes human maturity slower to accept "reality" for what it is. Someone wiser than me said, "more suffering comes into the world by people taking offence than by people intending to give offence". Confidence has to be nurtured in childhood for people to find their true identity and to avoid negative attitudes. This helps reduce anxiety and fear especially when changes have to occur in moving house or school. Personalities and self image are formed early in life with our relationships and experiences which contribute to making us unique individuals.

WHAT IS LIFE

Life is opportunity, seek it.

Life is a duty, complete it.

Life is costly, care for it.

Life is love, live it.

Life is a promise, fulfill it.

Life is a song, sing it.

Life is a gift, enjoy it.

Life is beauty, admire it.

Life is a challenge, meet it.

Life is fun, play it.

Life is wealth, share it.

Life is mystery, believe it.

Life is tragedy, confront it.

Life is sorrow, overcome it.

Life is a struggle, accept it.

Life is an adventure, dare it.

Life is a Blessing, know it.

Life is precious, do not destroy it.

My Acronym for L.I.F.E. means "Living In Faithful Eternity"

Chapter 2

CREATING ENERGY WITH IMAGINATION

Romans 15: 5

E.N.E.R.G.Y. Eternal Necessary Effort Rewards Growing Youth

What are some of the basic requirements to be a well balanced person, Mother or Father to a child or children, as a creative parent with imagination? To fulfill our human role of being co-creators with God we need to be living a Life of Valuable Energy [Love]. I will start with Fathers because I believe boys have been missing out for decades. I have met many men in the Mining Industry, in Society and Parish life who did not have a good caring, guiding relationship with their father. Absentee fathers not only in the Mining Industry, in the Police Force, Military Force, Doctors, Lawyers, Politicians with excessive work loads, also many others who think drinking with their friends after work more important than playing with their children, especially boys.

To live a Life of Valuable Energy, means knowing yourself to have the confidence, courage, creativity to communicate with commitment when we take on the most responsible, rewarding job in our life—fatherhood. No matter how good you are in other fields of life, to fail with your Son means not only your loss, but a loss to the community and for the contribution they could make to Society.

This also endangers their ability to be a good Father, plus a risk to their mental and physical health. All children should know they are valued, particularly boys by their Father. I believe this starts at the cradle and must continue through their young years and teens, so they arrive as young adults with confidence in themselves and what their choices are for their life. Not confused young men who do not see any future and want to commit suicide, for lack of their understanding their true value as a male human being. Some manage to get through the rough times, but are left with a lot of deep sub-conscious anger, that comes to the surface when they can't get what they want and end up taking revenge on family or other people.

Women can give compassion and care to their sons, but they cannot teach them their value as a male. That is one of gentleness and strength, when they understand there is nothing as strong as gentleness and nothing as gentle as real strength, which gives a well balanced creative, energy and power. This works wonders with women, children and men, a great example Tim Fischer. Women and men should be complementary to each other and sharing their gifts and abilities for the benefit of each other, and sharing the load during the tough times. There is no limit to our imagination when we acknowledge the valuable energy we have to create joy and happiness in our lives. Boys should be raised with gentleness and strength and taught how to withhold gratification by their fathers, as they are growing and maturing so this does not come as a surprise when the male hormones kick in when they reach their teens to understand the true meaning of saying NO to themselves and where it has its place with girls in Society. The younger the boys learn this, the more their life becomes one of valuable energy, and how to manage their life. Truly Mothers cannot teach their boys this. A well balanced caring Father is required for all boys to be raised to be a credit to themselves and the community. Then they mature and develop a marriage rooted in mutual care and happiness for themselves and their Spouse as they care for each others needs. A similar training is also required for girls to understand themselves, their abilities and weaknesses and their life choices. It is very beneficial for boys to have some understanding of how women think, and also for girls to realize that they think differently to boys. This creative work is how both boys and girls should be raised, so they can start talking and communicating with questions that help them understand each other.

When we make a marriage vow our hope and intention is we are going to create a new human Being with God's Gift of Love [Life of Valued Energy] Love is not a feeling, it is a decision of our will, to bring into the world a Life of Valuable Energy with responsible, disciplined freedom and guided imagination. They know how they arrived with their parents but not where they have come from, the human Spirit is part of our Puzzle. When this vow and choice is freely made their pledge is fidelity and they become one flesh leaving their Mother and Father. This union is that they marry each other required by Law. If they wish to have God's Blessing they can be married in a Church of their choice. Some will have a Christian background. Some may have no faith or religious belief, however it is important to understand that the people of most other cultures and churches have a partly developed understanding of God even if they are not practicing their religion. Sexual intimacy is not only for procreation of the human race. It is also for a deepening of our imagination of a Life of Valued Energy for the chosen commitment that a husband and wife have for each other and if also raising children.

A Father who has created with Love [Life Of Valuable Energy] and faith and a Christian sense of seeing himself as a co-creator with God to enrich further generations, needs a gentle strength, and a disciplined well balanced training of boys from the cradle to adulthood. As man does creative things with nature like building houses and growing food, so God gives humankind a share with creative imagination. This Divine creativity of Spirit is fed into the physical and spiritual life of their children. It is a great Blessing God gives us to share in Gods creativity of life. Wives with their husbands or partners enjoy receiving this Blessing of children, but also bare the pain of delivering this gift of life. This is only the beginning of having the pleasure plus the responsibility of parenting, and raising up God's gracious Gift. This is sometimes called a trusted endeavour to build a temple for a new image of God.

If Fathers and Mothers have lost the ability to create with imagination, a stable, caring and joyous home, the children will not be able to grow their physical, mental and spiritual health required to cope with this ever changing world. If they grow up with confusion and disillusion, it will be transferred into society, and become the negative Fear that is destroying lives now. All humankind, regardless of faith or culture must make decisions for an understanding that there "is nothing as strong as gentleness and nothing as gentle as real strength". This is not a weakness it becomes a well balanced power with creative energy for imagination. This enables us all to find stability and peace for our own and future generations to move through life without excessive stress of our own making. We are creating our own problems and diseases, and it does not help or heal by blaming anyone else or God. We are Blessed with God's valuable energy to turn our life into a life that Thrives not just Survives. It starts right now with you and me.

All well balanced, caring family life does not just happen by accident. It requires a good work ethic. It is hard work with good order, mutual love and respect. It raises the question, "what is our meaning and purpose for living?". For me it brings fresh new ideas and challenges for learning and creating, exciting and joyful experiences of life by using our imagination. Sadly there are still situations when girls are forced by parents to be married to a man they do not know or have consented to marry, and object strongly. This I believe changes the situation to forced abuse. The children created in this cruel process are still cared for by God, even when the marriage through awful rape falls apart, God knows the situation. When controlling fathers cancel their daughters application for further education and take their freedom of choice and autonomy from them, this was my experience and I tell this so abused women can get Justice. A wonderful Doctor got help for me and an operation so I survived, to raise and educate 3 girls on my own, teaching them independence and freedom of choice. Women should be free to marry or not marry, to have children or not have children, and no man or woman should rule over the other. Well balanced relationships should have tender, care and compassionate responsibility with true valuable appreciation for each other.

Now I am back to the Cradle as we are first gifted with valuable energy and the necessity of learning our Ethics at a very young age. If our parents or guardians listen and teach us when young it is a reward for both the child and the parent. Energy is part of our emotion and E-Motion is energy in action. It has been said in recent Centuries the study of mental issues and source of moral awareness of Christian morality is unified from its base of love made possible by God's Grace. This moral awareness applies to non-Christians as well.

Abuse in Domestic Violence.

If you have received sexual or any other type of violent treatment, learn you cannot control abuse, it is not your fault and no one deserves to be abused mentally, physically or spiritually. Do not wait too long to get out and find help. Men who use fear, anger and abuse to control have not been trained or learned to care and respect themselves and others in their youth. They may have received abuse and believe that is how they control others. You cannot change them they have to get experienced trained help to change themselves. It is hard work takes time, patience and courage. Sadly many men do not have the confidence and courage to change. This is what this book is about boys and some girls have not been taught their value from the Cradle and it is often too late to change. This can often happen after intimate relationships are developed so it is wise to do some self-discovery to avoid hidden attitudes before relationships start. Then do not let feelings get in the way of making important decisions for your life to avoid domestic violence. Feelings are important and should come after good decisions.

We humans waste our energy in many and various ways on this wonderful planet. The major way is Laziness. This is happening in the home, in the work place and the Corporations and Leaders of the world. We are lazy by the way we blame others and do not take responsibility for our ignorance and neglect of truth and our poor decisions. Too many people use the word 'love' as a feeling, when in fact it is a decision of their will and can have consequences by applying feelings without truthful and caring thoughts. For example the human race is constantly searching for valuable energy from the earth or the atmosphere. However much is done and said with lack of Vision of the consequences. Thus lack of valuable vision for life decisions can be sad consequences of domestic violence. My reason for search and seeking is my deep love of life and concern for the present parents and the future of the next generations for learning how to live with Love and without irrational fear to find a well balanced and shared life of gentle strength, confidence and creativity with greatly improved learned communication skills. I believe Skilled Parenting should be learned and nurtured from the Cradle for both the Parents and children for a healthy, happy God guided life. Governments are not voted in to raise our children it is totally our male and female Freedom which for me means For Responsible Energy Enables Discipline of Mind.

Chapter 3

CONNECTING WITH PRAYER

Matthew 6:5-15 Mark 11:22-25

P.R.A.Y.E.R. Praise Rendered After Your Eternal Reward

It is not for us to wonder why
Our friends and family say good-bye
We are born to live and to
Learn how to die, as Prayer connects us to God.

From the time we are born we are growing our life skills. By the time we are about 8 -10 years old we should be living an active, imaginative and healthy life. Seeking and searching, through our education and social learning the things that most interest us, and how we can apply our valuable energy to them.

Hopefully with parental understanding, you now enter another stage and begin connecting the changes that your mental capacity is developing. Leading to discovery and developing your mental and physical gifts. Of dreaming of what and how exciting life is and will be, with the challenges of your choices. Of growing up what ever your choices may be of musical, sporting, inventing, teaching, caring, helping talents with learning in all aspects of life. As we are growing there are many aspects of things that happen in our life that surprise and sometimes scare us.

When talking and communicating with other people we try to engage their thoughts and ideas which are often different from what we think and want. This can be what I call the "fear factor", which makes us uncomfortable when people or friends do not agree with us. Most of our fears are formed in our childhood, and we need to be aware we do not bury them in our heart to build up later in life, which can turn into anger when older. While young we need help to ask ourselves what we are fearful of, and when we talk about our fears we usually find they are not as bad as we first thought. It is important to begin to learn while young that no one can make us SAD, MAD OR GLAD, we each make our self disappointed-sad, angry-mad or happy-glad, it is our feelings. Our feelings are important, and when we are Glad we can be happy, joyful, funny, useful, helpful or playful. When we are Mad we feel angry, frustrated, annoyed, irritated, jealous, scared, impatient and fearful, which can make us tense, anxious, worry, nervous, insecure and can lead to depression [often undetected in small children].

The word LOVE, previously mentioned in this book, is NOT a feeling. It is a decision of our WILL, the same for the word FORGIVENESS, it is not a feeling it is a decision of our will. I will connect this amazing word to many appropriate situations in life in chapter 6.

Discovering Prayer

There are as many ways of praying as there are people who pray. We believe that we pray but in fact it is the Holy Spirit that infuses our Soul that leads us in prayer, and forms a bond with God 2 Cor.3:18 before we have time to articulate our prayers God knows our needs. Mtt.6: 8 Then we are led into a state of inner quiet and silence. This Silence is Contemplative Prayer, so we are aware of the Divine will, and listen with our heart, mind and soul. This also brings us to the Spirit of those we are praying for healing. When we try to express communion with God in words, we rapidly reach the end of our capacities. But in the depths of our Being Christ is praying, far more than we imagine. Compared to the immensity of that hidden prayer of Christ in us, our explicit praying dwindles to almost nothing. That is why Silence is so essential in discovering the heart of Prayer. Although God never stops trying to communicate with us, God never wants to impose anything on us. Often God's voice comes in a whisper, in a breath of silence. Remaining in silence in God's presence, open to the Spirit, is already prayer. It is not a matter of trying to obtain inner silence at all costs by following some method that creates a kind of emptiness within. The important thing is a child like attitude of trust by which we allow Christ to pray within us silently, then one day, we will discover that the depths of our Being are inhabited by a Presence.

Often our prayers are answered with God's will which may be different from our will. God's healing sees into the heart when we might be looking for a physical sign. We look for relief of pain but God maybe looking for a transformed person. Isa.55:8-9 "my thoughts are not your thoughts and your ways are not my ways." To be an agent of healing we need to have unconditional love for God with all our Being, and for our neighbour as our self, to fill the person who is suffering with God's Spirit. Then supported by God's loving arms, our Spirit inspires the Soul and the Soul infuses the mind and renews the Body. When praying for my healing I find it more helpful to pray for God's love, compassion and strength to cope with what ever life throws at me, rather than any particular ailment or problem, for friends and family that they are unconditionally loved and gain a heartfelt bond with the Spirit of God. Then healing will come in God's time and often through other people, seen in hindsight, to bring relief from suffering and pain. It is well documented that suffering is part of being human, and we tend to blame God for allowing or not intervening to prevent our tragedies, which are mainly our own creation and responsibility. We need to be aware that God does not make our choices, we make our own. It is also people without faith that need our prayers as well as our elders in society struggling with fear and depression.

Fortunately for us who have faith Christ's help is available to those who ask and trust our Lord and receive the Peace of God that passes all understanding and gives us purpose in Prayer.

These days there are a large number of older members in society who have lost some physical energy and can offer some deep faithful prayer, particularly for the future of our planet and encouragement for the present generations to make good choices for our world. This includes removing the negative psychic atmosphere that is being a fear filled invasion of our world. Then we can bond with the Holy Spirit that has to penetrate the negative spiritual powers to energize and guide our world into a new resurrected life. Then the Spirit of Christ who gave up His life to save the world will transform and cleanse the minds of the leaders of the Nations.

Prayers of the Children

As a child my mother would read passages from the Bible to me and one I remember very well was Ecclesiastes 3: 1-8.in the Old Testament because the seasons were so relevant to me in the Queensland bush. Today I think another line could be added "a time for others and a time for self " [which Jesus did] "to love our neighbour as our self ". Because over the years I have found it is important to have quality time for self and then I can be truly effective for others. The younger we learn about God even though they may not yet understand their Spirit. We learn God's Presence is with us even though we cannot see Him / Her. Teaching children about the wind and air, I call God's breath that we can feel with our bodies but cannot see. This embraces the Spiritual Presence of God with our own Spirit. To help children to understand the awe and many wonders of Creation, this is prayer in Silence with God. This is helping them to be thankful for those people, toys or pets and the things they are discovering as they are growing up.

God is ready and waiting for us, we have to come to God with hope and trust, as we feel our prayer rather than thinking what to say. Then we receive and know God dwells in the Spirit 1 Cor.3:16-

17. This Spiritual balance is the Incarnation of God into Flesh John 1:14 and I use breathing exercises, others use walking and some use yoga as helpful. Read Philipians 2 :6-11 as this is thought to be an early Christian Hymn to the Christian Community to be a path of self-empting [kenosis] and considered a guide for the process to Contemplative prayer and our Soul [Spirit]. The Mystery Puzzle that is in us as we search out the missing pieces, this is why Jesus tells us to "follow Him" to find the Divine state in our True Self as we continue our journey. {more in Chapter 9}. When we accept that Jesus was not only human but Divine as well we begin to see we are not separate from Jesus. Help your self recognize the paradoxes in Jesus, which means understanding the truth of something that seems a contradiction. For example it seems a contradiction that Jesus is both human and Divine and that God is One also Three in One [Father Son and Holy Spirit] We must learn to accept paradoxes as in the Trinity and Reality it is life. We humans are a paradox [body mind and spirit].

There is nothing on this created earth that is not a mixture of good and bad at the same time, helpful and unhelpful, pleasing and maddening, living and dying. Paradox is hidden and obvious this is part of the Mystery of God's Creation, as we humans are all a mixed Blessing. Even Jesus said to the rich young man "why do you call me good? God alone is good". I believe heaven and hell are something that happens when life begins this can be Reality in various conditions. We should not consider we get rewards for being good, nor hell as being punishment for being bad. Heaven cannot be earned for our human behaviour, it is a gift like love and freedom.

The concept of reward and punishment implies God only loves us when we are good. That says God is a vindictive Being—that is not so—as God is Love. We humans are the ones who get vindictive and try to Blame God. Hell is what a person feels like or experiences it is not a place we are sent: it is the bad experience we have from the incorrect use of our freedom. I like many people have experienced both heaven and hell on this earth. Heaven is what a person feels like not a reward for good behaviour but a state of being of love and joy then we can say we are in heaven the consequences of the good use of our freedom.

Some people cannot forgive certain parts of themselves [dualistic thinking] they do not believe God dwells within them as 1Cor.3:16-17 states. This lack of forgiveness shows a tortured mind, or closed heart and totally uncomfortable in their own body, which creates Feelings Envy Anger Revenge which is Fear. With non-dualistic thinking we mend and renew ourselves by strengthening our response.

1. When we want others to be more loving, choose to love them first.

2. If wanting peace first create it in our self.

3. If you want justice, treat your self justly too.

4. When resenting other peoples faults stop resenting your own.

5. If the world seems desperate let go of your own despair.

6. If you want to find God, then honor God within you. For it is God within you that knows where and how to look for God. Jesus said the same thing in Luke 6:36-38. Do not judge and you will not be judged, do not condemn and you will not be condemned. Forgive and you will be forgiven. Give and it will be given to you. Now you will understand Matthew 7:8.

Mohandas Gandhi said, "be the change you want to see in the world" When we recognize our Spiritual image within our self, we cannot help but see it in everyone else and we know it is just as undeserved and unearned as it is in us. This is why we stop judging and start loving unconditionally without questioning their worthiness. This leads us to a deeper connecting with God. Paul warned us in 1 Cor.1:19-31 that without knowing it most of us are educated in Greek logic. This is through measurements such as A is not B, both are different and cannot be A and B at the same time.

Consequently this dualistic thinking has difficulty when it comes to including the third factor C. As Christians we understand Father Son and Holy Spirit to form the Trinity of 3 in 1 as a single Being. We ourselves are a Trinity of body, mind and spirit. This makes for all people including Christians a Puzzle, to find the missing pieces we need to grow to include in our understanding the third factor we know as Spirit that leads to a non-dualistic Blessing given to us by the Mystics, the early Theologians. When we know God's Spirit is in us and things in the Universe seem to have lots of impossibilities which are paradoxical and mysterious for examples black holes and neutrinos. Science tells us these things cannot be measured, they are there but no one can prove it. Most adults have heard how light is both a wave and a particle, and is clearly both at the same time. So we need to allow our Theology blend with Science and move ahead until more of the Mystery of our Spirit can be discovered.

Many Christians want Certainty all the way, without honest study suffering, waiting and developing our inner journey. They just want to think their way to God while still calling it Faith. When we have a humble trust and hope we can call it true Faith. The Lord our God is one Deut. 6:4. The non-dualistic paradox and Mystery for Christians is Jesus truly human truly Divine Heb.12:23 consistently calling us to" follow Him" all the gaps are overcome and the Cosmic Universe misunderstanding as Paul in Col.1:15-23 tells us. It has been said we have decided to make Jesus a Religion and worship Him, instead of following Him on our Journey to God. When we accept Jesus is not only Divine but human as well, we can accept and see how we are not separate from Jesus, and can hold opposites in tension within our self. You may well ask, how do we correctly see? We need to be fully aware, without fear or judgment. It is hard work for those to let go of their Ego and emotions so the body can find the non-dualistic contemplative life. In Matt 6:22 Jesus is referring to our inner eyes connecting us to Prayer.

Chapter 4

DECEIVING OURSELF AND LYING IS EVIL

Matthew 5:43-45.and Genesis 2:9

E.V.I.L. Energy Violent in Life

Sensitivity to the truth from my experience means listening, to the language being used, for harmony, negativity or complicated terminology for abuse. Jesus taught in Aramaic the common language spoken by the people, to help everyone understand, not only the educated few. I use the pronouns of masculine and feminine He/Her because I believe God created Himself, as a masculine Being Jesus to work in a masculine world, where women and children were second class citizens. Jesus also had feminine attributes of gentleness, kindness and compassion and specifically criticized the men for the way they treated the disabled, the young and the women in their culture and society. We also have both masculine and feminine attributes.

I use the words "we" and "us" to mean human beings in general. Our English language can at times be confusing, such as using the term "3 persons" when referring to "God Jesus and Holy Spirit", which means separate identities. Also saying "Jesus sitting at the right hand of God", when Jesus returned to being God and sending the Holy Spirit to us.

These and other words often confuse meaning in the interpretation of one language to another, from Aramaic to Hebrew, to Greek, to Latin to English. Another word is "perfect" used in Matt.5:48 not existing in the Hebrew or Aramaic language, so Jesus did not use that word. There are several other passages that scare people, and are not always culture, correctly related to us today. Such as Matt.25:46 and Matt.5:29. These passages portray a violent, unloving and untrusting God and have no parallel in the other Gospels. According to some Theologians it would seem Matthew added them. Why? It was an expression of threats that Matthew heaped on the Pharisees. Matthew and his community, it appears were doing to the Pharisees , who did not follow Jesus, what the Pharisees were doing to them. The reason being after an unsuccessful revolt against Rome in 70AD, the Pharisees believed God [the Pharisees followed Old Testament] was punishing them for allowing the followers of Jesus to worship in their Synagogues, and put out prayers and a petition asking God that Jesus followers should perish. So the response from Jesus' Disciples was threats that God consign the Scribes and Pharisees to hell. Matt.23:15, 33.

Many Theologians acknowledge the fundamental message in the Bible is that God loves us and can be trusted. Thus the final revelation in John.20:21-23 is God of Peace breathing on the Disciples, and is identified as being a nonviolent God of forgiveness. Jesus most consistent teaching in the New Testament is one of unconditional love [Life Of Valuable Energy] gifted at our birth. We are to use this Gift to follow Him/Her with the recipes we are given in His teachings and parables. Rather than punishing them the risen Jesus in Matt.28:20 forgives them even for deserting Him saying "I am with you always, yes to the end of the age". In Luke 23:34 with His final words on the Cross "forgive them they know not what they are doing". In Mark there is no mention of punishment. In John21:9-12 Jesus appears to them by the Sea of Galilee by inviting them to breakfast. There seems to me to be cultural differences in Jesus time, that can confuse us. However there are some similarities with our Global nations even today.

The Bible includes History, Biography and Poetry, some of it is symbolic, and I believe His Parables to speak truths beyond rational understanding. I believe much of this teaching has deep psychological meaning, when we learn the culture and time in history to which the stories and parables refer. I like the story about one theologian teaching some Nuns about Hell. One Nun asked him about the Sheep and Goats Parable where the sheep go to heaven and the goats go to hell. He responded with 2 questions. How many of you have fed the hungry, clothed a naked person or visited someone in prison? All put up their hands. He said "that is wonderful you are all sheep". Then he said "how many of you have walked by a hungry person, failed to cloth a person who needed it, or not visited some one in prison?" Then slowly they all raised their hands. He answered "that is too bad you are all goats". Then an old Nun put up her hand and said "that means we are all Good Goats". That Nun did understand heaven and hell are not geographical places we are sent. Rather they are symbols for states of being that all of us have experienced. Whenever we feel alienated, overwhelmed by shame, or helplessly caught in addiction, we have experienced Hell. Whenever we have been welcomed home or healed by a Doctor into recovery we have experienced Heaven. Heaven is acceptance, union, and being valued we have all been in Heaven and in Hell. We are all sheep and goats, and have wheat and weeds in us. Perhaps one meaning of Matthew 25 is that the Kingdom of God is within us and we are all good goats.

Jesus' mental attitudes, and physical examples of teaching is unconditional to the Life of Valuable Energy we have been gifted. Jesus only gets angry when the educated Scribes and Pharisees think and act their unbelief and use ways to corrupt the people. He points out suffering is inevitable and life is difficult. When we accept life can be difficult even tragic, we are challenged to work through the situation. This requires Disciplined Freedom to make our choices, and discover the Truth of Reality. Once we learn our complaints and problems can be solved with gentle and strong discipline the pain of conflict is less confronting. Once the demanding difficulties born out of Fear cause grief, sadness, guilt or anger, anxiety or despair are recognized, the uncomfortable feelings can be overcome with courage. By meeting problems and solving them, we find a meaning in life and grow mentally and spiritually. I hope we can teach and encourage our children in this process to hear problems and not avoid them. There are many older people who have not learnt this when younger and then avoid problems with emotional suffering and this becomes a tendency to deceive our self. Darkness is a metaphor for "evil".

E.V.I.L. these letters stand for "Energy Violent In Life" all our feelings of negative words stem from the root word "Evil" –fear, envy, anger, revenge, rage, jealousy, disobedience, annoyance, hatred, frustration and selfishness no doubt you can add to the list. These are some of the evil feelings and any other words that are destructive to our thinking and actions. Our mind is not evil no force of nature is evil. C. S. Lewis said "the devil will not appear with a fork and horns but in a three piece suit".

The problem of evil is we know it is Real and not just our imagination or a religious up bringing. There are some people who set out to respond with hatred and destroy any good they see being achieved. A community example is new tree plantings are pulled out of the ground in anger or envy, even when they are not aware of the event of evil in their Soul, because it is a fun thing to do. This is a deep sense of Fear and rejection and wanting attention. They avoid self-awareness of their actions because they hate goodness that reveals their laziness to consider self-awareness. This evil has been defined as the opposite to love [life of valued energy] because it is their failure to extend themselves to help others, even themselves. They are known to protect their own laziness, and this is the evil called anti-love. Because humans possess Free Will it is inevitable that some people attain more evil in them than others. Evil and Valuable Energy are opposing forces. It can be used to destroy the hearts and minds of young people. Fortunately most of us have been Graced by the horror of evil when we recognize its presence and aware of its existence. Many people think of Heaven and Hell as places where we go when we die, when life ends. I believe heaven and hell are something that happens when life begins. This can be reality in various conditions. We should not consider we get reward for being good, nor hell as being a punishment for being bad. Heaven cannot be earned for our human behaviour. It is a gift like love and freedom. The concept of reward and punishment implies God only loves us when we are good. That says God is a vindictive Being – that is not so – as God is Love. We humans are the ones who get vindictive and try to blame God. Hell is what a person feels like or experiences, it is not a place we are sent: it is the bad experience we have from the incorrect use of our freedom. I like many people have experienced both heaven and hell on this earth. Heaven is what a person is like not a reward for good behaviour, but the consequences of good use of our freedom that is a state of Being of Love and Joy we can feel we are in Heaven.

Chapter 5

FEAR IS JUDGING, BLAMING AND SUFFERING

Matthew 7:1-2. Mark 6:50. Genesis 3:8-14

F.E.A.R. Feelings Envy Anger Revenge

Christ made it clear that humans cannot save themselves by the "letter of the Law", but salvation of Eternal Life comes with co-operation with God and the "Spirit of the Law". Jesus said he came to fulfill the promises of the Old Testament Prophets, to enter the Kingdom of God. To love God first and neighbours as our self were to be the two greatest commandments. Making judgments of others was the result of their sins causing blame and suffering, instead of using the power of LOVE {God's life of valued energy} to relieve their pain.

Christ was teaching the process through which the stages of human development must pass, with greater emphasis on friendship than blood relationships. So the process of development of each individual cannot be allowed to continue in a state of chaos or destruction for too long. God's guidance of "good order" is necessary for survival. Law is not the only basis for order, and without this sensitivity, freedom can become dangerous, and responsibility must be properly understood. Christianity is not a religion of law and rules but one of Love and Responsibility to do 'good' and avoid judging, blaming and suffering.

Judging and blaming causes disunity and suffering. The use of judgment in a negative sense is the desire to create distance from another person. It usually implies rejection of a certain relationship. A person of criminal behaviour is usually removed from society and imprisoned. A child thrown out of home by parents is also being judged. In practical terms "judgment" is meaningless without impact, unless it diminishes or changes behaviour in some way. In the Bible the word 'judge' sometimes refers to drawing conclusions about a person instead of a particular action. It was in this context that Christ warned us when He said, "judge not and you shall not be judged". This clearly means not to evaluate a person with our limited knowledge.

Justice, compensation and mercy, is whenever people fail in their responsibility they do an injustice to us for which we are entitled to adequate compensation. The consequences of injustice are usually some form of judgment while uncorrected. In our demand for justice, Mercy is our restraint to be prepared to offer forgiveness. Forgiveness is an expression of Faith and Hope that unity can replace division. Guilt and reconciliation feelings have a useful and appropriate role where a person behaves contrary to their informed conscience. When a genuine reason to feel guilt we should seek reconciliation, whether it be God, another human Being or our self. As well as being forgiven by others we must learn to forgive our self. Suffering plays a vital role in our growth into deeper awareness and the source of this awareness is to be found in our self. Many people look for outer sources of relief such as economic or health projects, these only scratch the surface. The cause lies deep in our humanity. The failure to face Reality is a symptom of a deeper disease or attitude. When the mind of man believes he/she is capable of solving all our problems and diseases through research, economics and social means. There is a need for God's Wisdom that comes from increasing awareness that is required to correctly relate human needs to self-assessment and relationship unity for human development. Thus full Spiritual insight is not yet attainable and suffering is seen as a result of disharmony between God's gift of the Holy Spirit and humanity. Those with a more reasoning mind and less of an Ego are able to respond to the Spirit of God and co-operate with it. MK.:10:17-18. This means their Will is awakened to a higher way of life, whose concern is for others beside themselves.

Pain in various forms is an amazing teacher of transforming power. For those who can stay its unnerving force with steadfast Faith, have the gift of the Holy Spirit and perhaps is a test of a life well spent with LOVE. I personally believe we all have our quota of pain to endure. ECCL.12:1-2. If we remember God with this intensity in our life, suffering will merge into happiness in John 8:31-32 Jesus said, "you dwell within this revelation, you will indeed be my disciples, you shall know the truth, and the truth shall set you free."

The Bible tells us life is difficult even tragic. It is a great truth, and once we truly understand it and accept it, life then becomes Love: life of valued energy, {LOVE is not a feeling} and problems will be approached with "Discipline" I call the LIFE partner of FREEDOM. This is the way to search HOW to solve our problems. Often with human moans and groans. Without discipline, we cannot solve anything, and it takes total discipline to solve everything, which very few humans acquire. As mentioned in Chapter 1, at our birth we start complaining leaving our comfort zone. Our sudden awareness "that life is not meant to be easy" but as added "but darling it can be delightful". However many problems can be painful and the process of meeting and solving problems can give us meaning to our life, as we are called to develop confidence to find courage, creativity to learn communication and commitment, to grow mentally and spiritually. Many of us attempt to avoid the pain and problems, rather than work through them. This can cause increasing pain and suffering, that had we found the courage to face the original difficulties, and experience legitimate suffering as a necessity towards real healing. For ourselves and our children let us teach the value to face problem solving to achieve mental and spiritual health, by learning and growing in the process. This is the benefit of teaching Discipline. This is four suggestions or ways of coping with suffering.

1. To delay pleasure, to cope with pain first, more rewarding.

2. To accept responsibility, nothing is solved unless we take responsibility to solve it.

3. To aim for the Truth.

4. To balance the positive and negative.

This is a process where pain is confronted and not avoided. Young children are easily taught this through playing games— you go first – eating their cake first and the icing last. Then doing homework first so can ride or play later. If they use the play now, and study later method they usually end up stopping learning which leads to a pattern of failure in relationships, accidents, psychiatric hospital or goal. If you had a parent who was a control freak," do as I say not as I do," and these children were frequently punished throughout their childhood, kicked, beaten, slapped or punched. This type of discipline is FEAR control because it is a way to make promises they don't keep---with their lives clearly in disorder. It does not make sense to children when father beats mother, then mother beats son for hurting daughter. This modeling makes no sense when boy told to control his temper a school. When parents behave in a certain way the young child sees it as the way it should be done. To spend time with them and care for them and watch a young child with their pet dog---train, feed, play with and hug; children show us their needs or an adult who likes their garden and how they spend time and energy caring for it.

The Grief Process

Shock/Denial	Acceptance/Relief
Emptiness	Sadness
Isolation	Grief
Fear	Irritable
Guilt	Anxiety
Shame	Anger
Anger	Solitude
Resentment	Emptiness
Bitterness	Numbness
Despair	

Suffering, to understand all is to forgive all. Prov.23:7 {King James}. When we understand the way our own mind works we stop blaming other people, and we think something good can come out of our suffering. We need to move our mind to freedom and peace of mind for a more constructive purpose. Part of life is suffering for all of us in different ways. For me the Holy Spirit, Love, Resurrection and Evil are real and can be either mental or physical. It has been said once we recognize Resurrection is within us it becomes the breath of Adam {human} Genesis.2:7 and is transformed to the breath of Jesus {Holy Spirit} John 20:22. Then no one will have control as Breath—Wind—Spirit "blows where it will" John 3:8. It is interesting that on most accounts it was the women who were at Jesus death and come to believe more quickly than the men. This I have found in my Ministry when visiting and caring for the sick and accompanying the dying. This has taught my life of valuable energy as well as my own suffering that Jesus showed us that Love is stronger than death Heb.12:2 and He is the perfecta and guarantee of our faith Heb.7:22 and that love works Eph.1:13-14 when planted in our heart. Jesus said in John 10:30 "I and the Father are one". The unique leader and Father of all humanity Eph.4:6.

The crucified Jesus stands with our humanity of suffering and tragedy promises our suffering will not be the final word. The risen Christ confirms that God's final word is Love and Mercy. The Gospels tell us His death had to be made visible and tragic, because humans want to deny death, and avoid pain and suffering, that is understandable but we have to accept the price of living and dying. Jesus was a pure gracious gift of Love a life of valuable energy and freedom to us. His birth in Bethlehem was God's unconditional choice and gift of Himself to us. For us Jesus did not come to change the mind of God about humanity, but to change the mind of humanity about God. As Einstein said "Great truth would always have to be simple and beautiful."

Jesus' death was revealing our own human problem of FEAR and we kill what and who we should love. What do we fear most of all? Perhaps we fear the way to Resurrection, to be transformed through the gate we must pass through and to learn to die our final death, to know HOW to die and not be afraid. Then in trust the risen Christ's presence appears after we stop denying and blaming. Paul says in several places then our old self has been crucified Rom. 6:6. Then again in Rom 8 22-26 where we read natural Creation groans as do females in child birth. Suffering is a part of the cycle of life, when we experience the changing seasons of dying and renewing. The human cycle sadly often emulates the predators and prey of the natural world. Our Life Of Valuable Energy happens when there is true value in disciplined Freedom. This is the reality of God's message in human suffering.

We correctly question the terrible suffering caused by people in Christ's Church, from recent sexual failures and scandal "how can a good God allow this to happen" many people ask? I believe God gave us all a Life Of Valuable Energy, Love and Freedom of choice to learn How to be truly human and responsible for the care of all Creation, to give our life of valuable energy to be co-creators with God for the well being and benefit of our world. Evil is the hurdle we have to recognize and jump when life throws difficult challenges at us. This is when we trust God's Holy Spirit His help is available when we Ask and Listen a guiding message does come, to us or through another Believer. When we ignore God poor thinking and evil may be the consequences.

Carl Jung said "people need to accept that 'legitimate suffering' in the world comes from being human". There is the old message that "that life is hard" and consequently we are our own worst enemy when we deny this. I have used the Crucible Vessel as an example previously, which holds boiling metal to be purified and clarified. It has been suggested that the catholic [universal] Christian Church has to face its own boiling point at a much deeper level to survive and be set free to enter the Kingdom of God. Thus the Christian Church is a training ground for both human liberation and Divine Union. Forgiveness and suffering are necessary for learning being two main cycles in life. This is evident in the natural world with the changing seasons, the trees, all nature and animals living and dying. The violent storms and earthquakes and destructive fires are part of human suffering, then regeneration, back to life. This is the Freedom of Creation, the world in which we live and our human life of valuable energy needs a major overhaul of Divine help to re-connect with Love not Fear for God's Creation to survive and thrive.

Chapter 6

FAITH FORGIVENESS AND HEALING

John 12: 44-46 Hebrews 11

F.A.I.T.H. Forgiveness Asked In Truthful Hope

In my teenage years I found it easier to forgive others, than to accept forgiveness. When I came to know and feel I had been forgiven, it was the accepting of the forgiveness that put demands on me. It was then I had to respond to others by dying to self importance.

Desmond Tutu said, "Without forgiveness there is no future". God's ability to adjust to our failure is called God's mercy and compassion. God's forgiveness wants us to have the same relationship of forgiveness.

When we experience God's love we should trust and love God in return. The Gospels admit that life can be tragic, and then gives us the will and shows us how to survive and grow from tragedy. First we fall, then recover from the fall, both are the mercy and forgiveness of God. Jesus is not upset with sinners, only the people who think they are not sinners. Jesus looked for and found order out of disorder. That is why the truth of the Gospel still heals and renews all it touches, when we trust it.

The learning of forgiveness of everything is the growth of maturity and holiness. We need to understand any suffering we experience is not from God, but from our human failing of fear and anger, which requires a great deal of forgiveness of ourselves. The necessity for forgiveness is for healing, as painful as it may be for both the victim and the accuser. We cannot totally forget however we can totally FORGIVE. This means we have to come to terms and remember without pain. This often includes anger, and if we hang on to anger too long we continue to hurt ourselves. Some people say it is selfish forgiveness for our own sake. I believe it is self- care, even if the offenders never know they have been forgiven. If we hold on to our anger we stop growing and our SOUL will shrivel. Forgiveness is at the heart of the Gospel. Jesus demonstrated forgiveness at every level of life, healing the sick, freeing people from guilt and those who failed Him he forgave their sins .Luke 5:20; John 8:11; John 21:15-17and called on God to forgive those who nailed Him to the Cross.

We are to have forgiveness central to our way of life. This is not always evident, though God's offer of forgiveness through Christ is for all humanity. That I believe is the Good News from God the Good Judge. We humans are judgmental and require repentance for wrong doing or abuse. That involves being prepared to face the consequences, particularly abuse to children, this is the responsibility of all humans regardless of culture, race or religion.

We are told that in Baptism, the cleansing of our sin is washed away by the Holy Spirit. Jn.13:10 and in Christ we cannot sin. 1Jn.3:9. This is a process of inner purification which extends throughout life. That is why we must pray daily for the struggle against sin. Eph.4:22-32. This is based on God's Grace and is to be distinguished from man's resources. Also worship strengthens me through the Power of the Spirit that protects, comforts and upholds me in times of stress---not my own resources. You may well ask, "how do you perceive power?" Power is energy. It is either good or bad energy, constructive or destructive. Often people refer to power and they actually mean "authority". I believe we are gifted with God's energy [love] and I believe this is maintained and controlled by the strength God gives us through FAITH---TRUST and PRAYER. If we speak of power as in authority, we are only given that by others, such as "leadership" which has limited power, which is only the power of persuasion with responsibility. I believe I have authority for myself, but do not claim authority for others unless given to me. Even then I believe we are all under God's authority. I believe the only appropriate power in this world is "the power of good", which can and does flow through us when living a life of LOVE. This Good News is that Christ's power heals us and stops us distorting power over each other.

We must accept responsibility for a problem before we can solve it. Problems do not go away. They must be worked through or else they remain a barrier to growth of development and spirit. We have to be willing to take the time, to distinguish what we ARE and what we are NOT responsible for in this life. To perform the process adequately we must be willing to have the capacity to endure continual self—examination. If we follow God's commitments we will be internally free without anger, panic or worry. FREEDOM lies not in external circumstances, freedom resides in our heart. JN. 8:32----ROM. 6:18---GAL. 5:1 Freedom has a partner called DISCIPLINE where there is a paradox regarding freedom and thinking. On one hand we are free to think anything. To be healed we have to be FREE to be ourselves. However that does not mean we are free to impose criminal thoughts on others, or engage in destructive actions without consequences, with the freedom to think and feel, comes the responsibility to discipline our thoughts and feelings. Freedom without discipline can cause us great trouble. There is one poor thinking game that people play called "THE BLAME GAME". This is a repetitive interaction between two people with an unspoken payoff like manipulation [do it my way or else] stopping the Blame Game is called "forgiveness", because Blaming does not help or HEAL anyone. This is absolutely necessary for mental health. Blaming usually begins with anger and anger arises when we are criticized for our ideas or beliefs. Clearly we are to judge our self before we judge others. Jesus said," for whom much has been forgiven much more love there is to give". MK.11:24-26---EPH.4:31-32. The Biblical understanding of absolute forgiveness, once experienced should be enough to make us trust, seek and love

God. This integration or forgiveness of everything is the very name of growth, maturity and holiness. God being totally FREE to forgive all, even Bless God's own enemies, so He asked us through Jesus to Bless, Forgive and Heal. MTT. 5:43-48. God told us to love our enemies and all our Spirituality is to imitate God.

The Conscious and Sub—Conscious Mind

We only have one mind, that mind has two distinct working parts. When we think quietly and with conviction and sow positive thoughts of peace, kindness, gentleness, happiness and goodwill with our Conscious reasoning mind with what we believe to be the truth, we then plant these seeds of thought into our Sub-Conscious mind. Fill our sub-conscious mind with these thoughts Phil 4:8 tells us, because our sub-conscious mind is reactive and creative as it responds to the nature of our true conscious thoughts. We may need to change the interaction of the two natures of our mind if we want to change our thoughts or ideas. Then we must change the cause which is the way we chose our thoughts and images we want in our conscious mind.

Change occurs by overcoming one problem at a time. These problems are FEAR, SHAME and BLAME. We need to change our Belief system, and the first obstacle is to overcome our own unwillingness to change our MIND [our sub-conscious] to Listen and Co-operate with God, when our Belief system is based on FEAR rather than LOVE. I have heard a number of people [mainly men] say they had grown up without any models or training on forgiveness. Then as an adult had little awareness how important it can be, but considered it an abstract Religious concept. They then became experts in defending themselves and attacking others. We all need to understand HOW our MIND works. There are 2 sections--- the Conscious and the Sub-Conscious. Some people call it the Male and Female mind. I understand we all need the Conscious section for gaining Confidence and Courage for growing up our physical bodies to about the age of 30. Sadly many children are missing out on the more Gentle Sub—conscious training of FORGIVENESS and HEALING so vital for men and women to live a life of LOVE [L-for life—O-for of---V-valued---E- for energy] LOVE is not a FEELING it is a Free Choice of our Will, which means we VALUE a person for life, when you make a marriage or commitment VOW. This is often broken with lack of knowledge or training and this is when FORGIVENESS and HEALING ARE VERY IMPORTANT.

We all need to understand we can change HOW we think [mind] about how we can discover the Healing process. Our Ego [self-esteem] identifies totally with our physical body instead of recognizing ourselves as SPIRITUAL BEINGS who have come to live for a short time in a PHYSICAL body. When we are willing to change our THINKING and look upon ourselves as ETERNAL SPIRITUAL BEINGS; and not just as Bodies, it becomes much easier to see the VALUE of Forgiveness and Healing. Jesus healed anybody who asked for and desired to be healed. To be happy and peaceful we must learn the value of forgiveness and loving ourselves and others. When people hurt or deceive us we do not have to like their behaviour or actions. To love our enemies, is to heal ourselves and pray for God to change them. This can come about when we cease to look for someone to blame, when things go wrong in our lives. This is to surrender to Love instead of Fear. The unforgiving mind of the Ego has a stock of misery, pain, despair, suffering, and doubt, all coming from the root emotional word FEAR.

This can have a very negative effect on our thoughts, mind and health, such as headaches, ulcers, depression, anxiety, lack of energy, insomnia and unhappiness to name a few. Forgiveness is a powerful, amazing healer with the capacity for removing these symptoms. Forgiving others is the first step for forgiving ourselves. Forgiveness is a continuous process, not something we do just once or twice. It becomes easier to forgive when we choose to no longer believe we are victims.

The last thing our Egos want us to believe is that we have a choice. We can choose not to be victims, we can choose LOVE rather than FEAR. That we can chose to FORGIVE rather than hold onto our grudges and judgments. Forgiveness releases us from the painful past. My experience has been to use "writing" as a powerful tool in the process of forgiveness and healing relationships, a poem, a letter to a friend or an un-mailed letter to a person who has caused us pain or times of disaster. Also to someone who has died a letter saying what was left unsaid, is a way to express feelings that you found difficult to say before they died. Many people don't cry and express their emotions, and others cry a great deal and go on for months or years. There is no prescription for people to shed their grief, only unconditional love, acceptance and support.

We do not have to be in our bodies to communicate, our mind can communicate without a physical presence. When we have God's Holy Spirit we can choose to experience God's Presence when ever we wish. Also stress in our working lives, such as jealousies, fear of rejection, fear of being honest, sometimes these can cause problems and result in physical symptoms. Forgiving is the process of letting go to negative thoughts in our mind. It is the best way of healing our own mind and Soul, and an old Wisdom saying reminds us "when we have met the enemy, we find it is us", we call this being self—destructive. There is no set structure or form, as the person we forgive may never change at all. The major requirement is the willingness to change negative thoughts. This is the Freedom we have which is God's gift at our birth. Forgiveness puts us in the flow of Love and is the answer to all our problems. A few helpful reminders:

1. We are a Spiritual Being living in a Spiritual body.
2. Life and Love are Eternal.
3. There is no value in self-pity.
4. Chose to be happy rather than always "right".
5. Let go of being a "victim".
6. Unforgiving thoughts is a way for us to suffer.
7. Anger does not bring us what we want.
8. Make decisions based on Love not Fear.
9. Believe you deserve to be happy.

10. See people who are attacking us as fearful and looking for Help and Love.

11. Be willing to count our Blessings rather than our Hurts.

12. Believe that Forgiveness is the most powerful healing force in the world.

13. Accept the Love that others give you.

14. Remember the purpose of forgiveness is not to change the other person but to change the negative thoughts in our mind.

God pronounced everything Good and so should we. If we want to change our life, we have to change our mind. We have to fill our sub-conscious mind with the good thoughts and ideas we want to have in our life, and remove the unhelpful negative thoughts. Our desires of truth, justice, kindness, gentleness, peace, good health, security and happiness, the law of life is the law of belief which is a thought in our mind. When we think, feel and believe becomes the condition of our mind. It has often been said "what we think is what we say, what we say is what we do and what we do is who we are."

Jesus in the Gospel of Matthew 13:45-46 leads us to the price for healing. It is my experience that our health is taken for granted until we have survived a painful illness. It is my guess that "the pearl of great price" that we search for is good health and the good life, instead of the KINGDOM of GOD. In the search for the precious pearl, the seeker is led into strange adventures----material security, and emotional relationships, even religious conviction. It then follows that this Spiritual Journey being sought is renounced in order to acquire the precious article. As a rule for most of us we judge the value of an article by the price. We think that an article is of better quality if it is more expensive. It is a privilege as well as a responsibility to be born Human. Full Healing involves more than a surface improvement of suffering, essential as this may be in the short term. In fact the process of life is one of progressive healing.

This is the ministry of Faith, remembering that all of us progress by faith day by day and sudden flashes of light that illuminate the way, so we gain confidence to proceed onwards. The journey which is unique for each human is a small part of a well worn track trodden by humanity through the ages and Paul emphasizes the Love of God as a prerequisite for the working together for the good of all the strange, often confusing events in our lives. Relationships are the very basis of healing, in as much as the Holy Spirit works between Soul and Soul through the universal spirit shared by all Souls. While this love of God is a foundation for our healing journey, as we grow in our humanity to be able to accept the Divine revelation more completely. In other words the scales drop off our inner eyes with the result that, once we were inwardly blind, now we can see Spiritually. As a consequence, our Love of God grows stronger, we Love because God first loved us. In the healing process it is hardly a surprise that we look for a rapid release from our sufferings. In other words there is an unconscious self concern, rather than any love for God. This type of concern is natural but motivation is not so much as incorrect as inadequate. The younger this can occur, with training and loving guidance, the more fortunate we will be to find true happiness in life. Jesus told us to love God first and to love our neighbor as our self. This means we need to take care of our body, mind and spirit sufficiently before we can love anyone else in a similar manner. However self-love can far too easily become choked with personal desires, if we are not constantly and consistently inspired by the Holy Spirit that comes from God. So in the healing process we would be wise to commence giving ourselves over to God's love in trust. The more we strive for our self, the more we distance our self from others, as our private affairs dominate our life. Thus God does not interfere with the Freedom of choice with which He has endowed us.

In the world of Faith in the Christian, Jewish, Buddhist and Moslem religions all get answers to their prayers in spite of the differences among the Faiths. The followers answered prayer is the realization of our hearts desire. It has been said that it is not the thing that is believed that brings an answer to Prayer, it is answered when our sub-conscious mind responds to the mental thought in our mind. This is the Silent operating principle in all religions and the deeper reason for psychological truth. This is the power and wisdom found in our sub-conscious mind for knowledge and understanding that provides us with an open mind and receptive intelligence. Though invisible it helps us find the solutions to our problems and sets our mind and Spirit free.

I like to make some use of Principles of Science [which means the way things work] that are universal and unchangeable. Our sub-conscious mind is a principle and works according to the law of belief. Mark 11:24-25 "whatever you ask for in Prayer, believe that you have received it, and it will be yours". The law of our mind is the law of belief and belief is the thought of our mind, and this belief is what brings about the result. Stop accepting false opinions and fears that plague humankind, the sub-conscious mind sees without the use of natural vision but with our heart and emotions.

In the Bible Job said "what I feared has come upon me" all his negative thinking. So our negative thinking "I will catch the flu if others in the room or church sneeze" becomes a fear in our mind that creates what we fear and expect. Finding the missing pieces in our human puzzle is the healing method for our life of valuable energy. If we fill our sub-conscious with great truths our external actions will reflect them and bring peace and healing. It is time to develop a healthy respect with our thoughts with positive thinking. When we repeat positive thoughts again and again it becomes second nature. An example "an apple a day keeps the Doctor away" this is prayer on a higher principle, this is how we learn to walk, swim or how to play a musical instrument.

We have one mind and this has two sections, the Conscious is the objective master of our decisions and the Sub- Conscious is the store room or pantry and takes orders from the Conscious mind that what it believes to be true and is planted in the Sub-Conscious from previous experience such as our childhood.

If we say to our self "I cannot afford it" repeatedly" our sub-conscious mind accepts it and follows the order of the conscious decision that does not change, and applies to both positive and negative thoughts, if we change to negative thinking we lose the healing power. We are to remind our self that the healing power is in our sub-conscious mind like a seed planted in the ground. We are the Captain of our Soul our [sub-conscious mind] we have been given the freedom of our choice, choose God, Divine guidance health and happiness; choose life of valuable energy with confidence, courage, creativity, communication and commitment. This is the way our mind works when we think positive good will follow, when we think negative bad or unhelpful will follow. Our Conscious mind is our reasoning mind that chooses. Our Sub-Conscious accepts our ideas so selecting thoughts in our Conscious that Bless, Heal and Inspire that fill our Soul with Joy.

The Conscious mind has the power to reject suggestions that we do not require. We humans have our own fears, beliefs and opinions that we have acquired from our childhood. Some of them may be negative issues and less helpful and govern our lives unless corrected by our Conscious mind, do not finish a negative statement, reverse it immediately and change your life. We should then give our Sub-Conscious mind only those ideas that heal bless and inspire as the sub-conscious does not understand a joke. So we develop our sub-conscious mind with caring, joyful, healthy and positive values and ideas. Our mind is not Evil it depends how we use the powers of nature. There is no discord when the Conscious [visible objective] and Sub-Conscious [invisible subjective] are in harmony and work together. Then what we write on the Inside [sub-conscious] we experience on the Outside [Conscious] as in Heaven [our mind] as on earth [our body] and environment are in Balance. This truth was claimed by Moses, Isaiah, Jesus, Buddha and other Seers of the Ages. When we think negatively our frustrations are unfulfilled desire. With negative and destructive thoughts we generate these emotions and are often found in ulcers, heart trouble, tension and anxiety. We often damage or wound our self by getting fearful with jealousy, envy anger or revenge. These are poisons that enter our Sub-Conscious mind. We are not born with negative attitudes and many diseases originate in the Conscious mind and all healing requires Faith and positive attitudes in our Sub-Conscious mind. The Conscious mind does the planting of positive and healthy issues into the Sub-Conscious mind and is the power that completes the healing after a person's changed mental attitude. An old saying, "the Doctor dresses the wound but God heals it" as God has the power and according to our Faith "everything is possible for him who believes" Mark 9:23. "Ask and it will be given to you, seek and you will find, knock and the door will be opened to you." Matthew 7:7-8. When we pray we trust the law of healing, which is sometimes referred to as mental or psychological treatment or scientific prayer. This sub-conscious healing can be passed on to another person with the same Faith and understanding of the sub-conscious even when living at a distance. The fundamental principles of life are the process of a definite response of our creative mind to our mental thought and Spiritual belief. We must ask believing we will receive what image we ask for so our sub-conscious can make it productive with a feeling of joy in the completion of our desire. We can visualize in our mind's eye any picture we have in our mind is the substance of things hoped for as evidence of things not seen. Belief is a thought in our mind and what we think we create and a thankful technique is often recommended in the Bible by Paul. A thankful heart is close to the creative forces, causing many Blessings based on a Cosmic Law of action and reaction even before our prayers are answered.

In John 7:33-34 Jesus is saying good-bye to His Disciples from His earthly state to return home. He is telling them He will not be visible to them any more but has compassion for their physical and mental state and will send His healing power when we remember what He has said and done and ask in Faith for His healing power. Thus in Prayer and our sub-conscious mind we will receive His Holy Spirit for healing our desire. We can build health, happiness, harmony and peace by the thoughts we put in our mind. Our Sub-Conscious never sleeps and is always helping to keep us from harm. Our sub-conscious speaks to us through intuitions, hunches, urges and ideas. It is telling us to grow, advance, be brave and move forward. The urge to save lives through learning, compassion, kindness and justice comes from our positive valuable sub-conscious. Artists, musicians, poets, speakers and writers tune in with their sub-conscious powers and become inspired. Our Sub-Conscious mind is the store room of what is truth for us.

Jesus' parables and stories are leading us to follow Him and put our Gifts of Love and Freedom into our L.I.F.E [living in faithful eternity"] which we can call The Pearl Of Great Price.

Faith and Courage

Often people who suffer will ask themselves, "what have I done to deserve this" or "why me"? Usually a person who is aware of the Holy Spirit protection they have been given, can face their fear and problems with faith and courage. Although apprehension may persist they will not allow it to cripple their decisiveness. Often they will find the experience was not as bad as previously imagined and may even feel proud of having overcome their fear. Always the person who acts with faith and courage tempered with wisdom gains or learns something, and finds having taken a crucial step their development has completely changed their life.

When all is going well for us our Faith is triumphant, but it tends to wane disastrously when shadows cross our path. It is then we come to a deeper self knowledge. Many people's self knowledge is limited to their physical body, which is their focus of identity. In his book" the Pain That Heals," Martin Israel leads us to a deeper understanding of how suffering and pain lead us to Healing.

PHYSICAL PAIN is beneficial to us, in that it serves to draw our attention to the source of disease within us.

MENTAL AGONY with appalling emotional overtones is far more terrible than physical pain, because it cannot be communicated to most people. Another factor that leads to mental pain is unrelieved FEAR. As previously stated Fear is a terrible cause of human suffering, especially the Fear of rejection, and fear breeds anger. Fear also breeds Jealousy when we compare our lot with those apparently more fortunate than we are. Jealousy is the cancer of the Soul—it eats away all compassion and concern for others.

We don't want pain. We try to get rid of this pain by drinking, smoking, not eating or eating to excess, drugs or abusive sex. Then when we give up these harmful habits we go through withdrawal symptoms which cause us even worse pain. If we are prepared with God's help to hang in there and endure the pain we come through the experience to new life. That is what the Cross is all about. Christ endured physical, mental emotional humiliating pain to show us Resurrection on the other side of the Cross. If we do not recognize and accept the Cross in our life---accept the pain and struggle--- we will never know what Resurrection is like.

It should also be said that Fear like physical pain serves a beneficial function in as much it promotes awareness and caution in the face of the bitter experience of past mistakes. The Fear of God is indeed the beginning of Wisdom. The LOVE of GOD is the end of Fear. The whole purpose of life is indeed the "Pearl of Great Price" { MTT.13: 45-46.} is to know that transformation is "from the Fear of God to the Love of God". For me the "Price of Healing" is the acceptance of suffering anger and pain as the Pearl of Great Price. Then we are enabled to find our true identity in God. It is well to remember that anger is a normal emotion and is not the problem, it is how we use, deal with and manage the anger. Anger is a tool we can use for the good of mankind. Jesus was angry in the Temple. When used correctly, it is a strong force for Good NOT evil. The naked TRUTH is to recognize HOW we can use anger with God's Help as a beneficial tool to help others or our self.

Jesus parable "the Pearl of Great Price" is truly Forgiveness for Healing.

Also Listen to the Words of Kahlil Gibran.

Our pain is the breaking of the shell that encloses our understanding

And

Much of our pain is self chosen, therefore trust the physician— God

And drink His remedy in silence and tranquility.

There are basically two types of people, those who accept a spiritual world and those for whom God's existence is impossible.

This is called the psychic mind which includes communication between the mind and the world. The Spiritual mind with the supreme attitude of Love [life of valued energy] transmitted through the Holy Spirit to the human Soul for our reasoning and to feed our emotions, often through suffering. The Spiritually blind can have the scales lifted from their eyes [so to speak]. This requires a true understanding and awareness of REALITY sometimes called The Cloud of Unknowing, the often painful experience of letting go of the EGO. As Jesus tells us, "the one who keeps looking back is not fit for the Kingdom Of God" LK 9:62.

This shows us the process Jesus went through from accepting Baptism from John the Baptist and identifying his humanity. Then the Holy Spirit descended on Him and sent Him into the wilderness for forty days, where He experienced the darkness of sin {evil} over human life and Jesus triumph over spiritual warfare. As the Book of Job in the Bible affirms, Evil was created by God and without the constant trial between "good and evil" we cannot grow to the fullness of human life. This testing is for us to have a creative living relationship with God to know God's Spirit is with us. "As in Adam, all men die, so in Christ all will be brought to life." 1COR.15:22.

It has been said by others that the EGO is an essential servant of a full person, but is demonic as a master. In other words we have to let go of the Ego, before our True Self can be resurrected in our Soul. As Christ said, "He did not come to be served but to serve" indeed to give up His life as a ransom for many. MK.10:45 Truly each person has to try to repeat the life of Christ before we can fully know God again in JN.14:6. "No man comes to the Father except by me." In the paradox of great suffering we come to know God's great LOVE, so as we give love to the world, we open ourselves to God the source of all Love. 1JN.1:5 "God is light and in Him there is no darkness." So when we read ISAIAH 4:5-7 we realize that God makes both darkness [pain, sadness] and light for all Creation. So this is the reason for our Gift of Freedom of choice at our birth.

When we are guided and trained with LOVE [our life of valued energy] and given affection and compassion as small children from the cradle, all through our growing years, approximately 20 or so years [different for each person]. To the age of responsibility, making our own choice, we grow up our physical and partly our mental capacities. However we still have the growing up of the Spiritual component of our Being. If this has not been our experience, we need a good self assessment of our needs and attitudes, strengths and weaknesses and how we move forward in life. We may need a wake up call to REALITY and this can be a creative beginning to Healing.

Chapter 7

RELIGION SEEKING SEARCHING FOR MISSING PIECES

Matthew 9:6. and John 14:15-21.

R.E.L.I.G.I.O.N. Responsible Energy Living In God's Image Of Need.

What type of pieces are we seeking and searching for to make our puzzle. "The gate is small, and the way is narrow that leads to life, and only a few there are that find it". Matt. 7:13-14. points to our need for a discerning Spirit.

Christianity is not a closed book of answers, but a way of life, a foundation for building and a pathway of exploration. So to begin we need to search for the Truth. At first we need to understand that the whole truth is not found in any single part by itself, but is found in the unity and relatedness of everything. Meaning the truth is found in the great Scriptures, in nature, some in science, and some in mysticism. All have enlightenment and disappointment, for in each source there is truth but not the whole truth. Christianity embraces the truth what ever its source. In this sense it encompasses what is good in all Religions and in Science. Christianity is about life and happiness, and relates to the past, present and eternity. It deals with human strengths and weaknesses, ideals and reality. It is concerned with unity, progress, preservation, meaning and purpose of life.

This can begin anywhere, but we first need to appreciate the difference between the truth and a lie, and between authentic communication and intentional deception. Without these we are not sensitive enough to recognize the truth.

There are many reasons why people abandon any Faith or Religion, here are a few of the following:

1. Their problems are not solved.
2. Church services do not stimulate them.
3. People see hypocrisy among the clergy or the members.
4. They cannot see good effect in the lives of others.
5. They had unpleasant experiences.
6. They cannot accept the teaching or rules.
7. They do not get the proof they demand.
8. It fails to give adequate meaning and purpose for life.

For many people their rejection is mostly from lack of study of their religion deeply enough. Also misunderstand every organization that is run by humans has failings and limitations. How do we find the pieces to pursue happiness?

My first aim has been to try to get rid of all the negative attitudes I have listed above. I believe negative ATTITUDES damage homes, churches, business and human character. We have the Freedom of Choice regarding the attitudes we will embrace on a daily basis. We cannot change attitudes of other people. The only thing we can do is use our free choice with a positive attitude to make the day, our life and those around us a happier place for them and us. It has been said, that 10% of WHAT happens to us is life, and 90% is HOW we react to life. So with all of us, we are in charge of our attitudes in the circumstances of our failures and successes. The hopeful aim of us all is happiness and without the commitment to achieving it, life is devoid of direction and meaning. There are several elements that always need to be present and in balance. These are:-

1. Development; connected with education, change, progress, creativity and growth.

2. Unity: involves harmony, consistency, peace, integrity, security, meaning, truth and order.

3. Good Experiences: often in hindsight that are mostly beneficial, enjoyable and fun.

Much of our behaviour shows an awareness of the importance of these elements. Often our actions speak louder than our words. Hopefully we are taught early in life how to develop our life-skills and fitness, not only for survival, but to benefit from opportunities we will encounter. To expand our knowledge and imagination to unify what we learn. These VALUES form a major part of our education, training and discipline for our happiness. So development, unity and good experiences should be consistent with one another, or can place future happiness in serious jeopardy. Also over emphasizing one element and neglect the others can cause problems. Our human nature is our individual and collective ignorance because we do not know enough to guarantee happiness, unless we learn early in life to do self-assessment. When we use guesswork and desperation to make many important decisions, they may lead to unwelcome results, which can lead to a multitude of other weaknesses.

The means of GUIDANCE, the accumulated knowledge and wisdom of the older generations is sadly ignored by their children. Often they reject much of the advice of their elders and insist on the 'right' to seek their own experiences and make their own mistakes. In nearly all our relationships on going ignorance plays a major part with our fellow human beings, and conflicts within our self. This is called our "state of sin" which is a state of alienation, disharmony and disunity. It is not necessarily connected with guilt or "committing a sin". However it is the human condition we all inherit. Even if we do not accept the Biblical explanation, our relative disharmony with the rest of the world is a recognizable fact. We can change that in ourselves, our Free Choice. The search for fulfillment comes after our basic levels for survival, such as food, water, shelter, human contact and freedom from suffering are developed. We then turn our attention to other things that we believe will bring us pleasure.

Self-assessment /self-discovery is a vital part of progress towards our happiness. It increases our abilities to identify compatible relationships and awareness of our strengths and our limitations that help us to be more selective and consistent for our well being. This enables us to have a meaningful purpose in life and means we need to seek to broaden our awareness, beyond the needs of our own comfort zone. Christ's words "seek and you shall find" Matt. 7: 7—8.sends a message to us that when we actively seek we find what we are meant to find, when we have an open mind. This helps us to appreciate our interrelatedness and opportunities for work and connections in communities where we live. Then we discover our inner happiness when we are willing to co-operate with Christ's Wisdom, and then with commitment put it into practice, which helps to bring about any changes we discover are necessary. Then in the long term elements of character such as confidence, courage, creativity, faith and a sense of justice help build our character, and we become people who can be safely trusted, with communication and commitment. This becomes LOVE—LIFE OF VALUABLE ENERGY with the type of pieces we are searching for to make a healthy helpful life. The Good News of the Gospels is that Christ came to give humanity a PERSCRIPTION for living [one we need to take] a happy life and a promise of Eternal Life. The purpose of Christ's teaching is to make it possible for us all to reach our highest potential and purpose of existence. It is possible a piece of the puzzle is missing such as a Mentor who will care and guide you. I encourage you to seek and find a trust worthy Mentor to assist with self-assessment to continue developing your potential if this is the situation.

Chapter 8

FINDING WAY THROUGH DIFFICULT PASSAGES WITH PEACE

John 14:27 Romans 15:33 Mark 9:50

P.E.A.C.E. People Enrich And Care Equally.

The problem of proof is there is no such thing as proof in the absolute or universal sense. There is only evidence and experience. This is what every Legal system recognizes where verdicts are based on the concept "beyond reasonable doubt". If total irrefutable proof were demanded no-one would ever be found guilty of crime. Because evidence can vary in strength and reliability, come direct from personal experience or be words of another person. What is enough to persuade one person to believe is not necessarily enough for another. Proof is very personal, there are many variables.

1. Such as, many people may see a given event and believe it happened. Others may claim mass hallucination or some other plausible explanation.

2. People differ in their sensitivities, what is perceived may be fact or illusion.

3. One person may have a higher developed intellect that can accept or refute a refined argument, another not even understand it.

4. People who have an aversion to an idea will demand much stronger evidence, to persuade them against their inclinations.

5. For some people no evidence is acceptable unless it is scientific.

Proof and Belief in God.

The first Commandment advises not to make craven images of God. The warning may equally have been intended to include mental images in the form of fixed ideas. As with a parent or friend we can have an intimate personal relationship, but we must always remain aware of how little we know about them. With God this is especially true, as God does not fit into any man-made concept. God described himself to Moses. This can best be summed up in the words "I AM the GOD who IS". There are two questions I want to explore.

1. How do we know Scripture is the authentic words of God?

2. Can the existence of God be proven at all?

For me the existence of God or the authenticity of the Scriptures cannot be proven by one person to another. Myself, or any Author can convey their experience and abilities, perceptiveness and evidence. What I have encountered is strong enough to persuade me to have personal conviction. When Faith has real meaning, then it is the Bridge between the evidence. Faith and experience are complementary. All areas of present human knowledge are a combination of both. In our awareness of God there is a higher component of Faith.

Faith gives us the confidence to act despite our imperfect knowledge. Whether we recognize Faith or not, there is a component of faith in every decision we make and every action we take. If we were to require absolute certainty and complete understanding we would never act at all.

Fear and Faith

"Do not be afraid, only believe." Mark.5:36. Those who have had extreme experience can have no doubt as to the existence of Heaven and Hell, rather than places they are states of being human. Many people think of heaven and hell as a place we go when we die, when life on earth ends. I believe heaven and hell are something that happens when life begins. This can start with the reality of our birth in various conditions. We should not consider we get reward for being good, nor hell as being punishment for being bad. Heaven cannot be earned for our human behaviour. It is part of God's gifts of Love and Freedom.

The concept of reward and punishment implies God only loves us when we are good. That is saying God is a vindictive Being----that is not true----as God is Love. We humans are the ones who get vindictive and Blame God. Hell is what a person feels like or experiences, it is NOT a place we are sent; it is the bad experience we feel and have from the incorrect use of our Freedom. I like many people have experienced both hell and heaven on this earth. Heaven is what a person feels like, not a reward for good behaviour, but the consequences of good use of our gift of Freedom, that is a state of Being of Love and Joy, now we can say we are in Heaven.

Though hell and evil are closely related, it is clear that everything that is painful in the short term is not necessarily evil. Shakespeare said "there is no evil unless our thinking make it so" evil must be seen with a long term view. It is true, 'that what we think is what we say, what we say is what we do, what we do is who we are." To associate evil with painful experiences or unwelcome states of being uncomfortable, is a useful guide to the things we say, and things we do that we should avoid inflicting on others and ourselves. Perhaps the most accurate definition of Evil is a cause for unhappiness of a permanent or Eternal kind. It is likely our understanding of Evil differs from Gods perception because of our limited vision of the future.

The question often asked is, "How can God who is revealed as goodness and love, permit evil to exist?" We do not know enough about God to offer a satisfactory answer, only a few interesting observations.

1. There are various degrees of good and evil and sometimes practical decision making involves compromise.

2. Pain is sensitive and unwelcome. However we are told it appears essential for us to have the ability to feel pain for survival.

3. For instance, we cannot learn to "do good" freely if only good exists. Also without problem situations to control for ourselves and the environment, which is necessary for freedom.

4. Good and evil, like order and disorder are influenced by our values, aims and sensitivities. Because order and disorder are individual situations which can be difficult.

5. Most well founded generalizations have their exceptions. Also some people have accomplished great things because of their handicaps, and often regard their limitations as assets not liabilities.

6. So "good and evil" confusion can arise, when we try to make absolutes out of concepts.

Nevertheless whatever reasoning we use to explain the existence of evil, the possibility of becoming a victim remains very real. All we can do is seek ways to handle that possibility. It has been said that God seems to be totally into change, that we grow more by learning from our mistakes and changing, than by ignoring the opportunities to change. Also to be human is to change, and to be perfect is to have changed many times. One Theologian said, that great people keep adjusting to what life throws at them, with their hearts and minds open to Gods messages of being in us and around us. JOHN.14:1-20. This leads us to the Contemplative way of Faith that teaches us HOW to BELIEVE as well as WHAT to BELIEVE. The word FAITH means different things to different people. I quote briefly R.Rohr's classifications of what he means by faith.

1. Faith is an opening of our heart and mind for any new change or encounter.

2. This re-opening means letting go of old ideas and confusion to move to another level of awareness. This explains how doubt and faith are correlative terms.

3. Such change is necessary in all encounters, relationships, intellectual ideas and Divine thoughts. Our faith is not that dogmas or moral opinions are true. It is that our Faith is about ultimate Reality/ God/Jesus is with us and around us. So Jesus can heal us, when we trust God's Love in Jesus

4. This allows us to bypass dualistic thinking for a while, and not about renouncing our rational mind and come back to reason again.

5. This contemplative thinking and acting for the Mystery to be explored, so to speak, for a deeper meaning. [Contemplative means turning all negative words and actions into positive words and actions].

6. Once we have gained access to non-dualistic unity, all previous stages can be returned as needed, because our reasoning will have a new freedom and clarity. Our thinking does not need to be always right or self-sufficient. We can share our faith and accept others criticism and still confirm our faith and hope in us. 1 Peter 3:15. With gentleness and respect the Holy Spirit in us tells us that God will make that decision, not our judgment. Faith and reason are not opposites.

7. When we reach a further stage in thinking, our Spiritual life always includes the previous stages of our growth.

8. If we want to reach what Paul refers to as "meat" instead of spiritual "milk" 1 Cor.3:1-2 we need to move through the early stages. What Jesus means by "being a child" is referring to the "beginners mind" in faith. This is important to understand Jesus is not idealizing infantile pre-rational thinking. We can then see that trans-rational thinking is free and the pre- rational thinking is either scared or inexperienced or both.

9. This can be reasonable only to those with a childhood understanding of faith, and are now returning to gain a different level of awareness. Check out Paul's experience in his blindness in Acts. 9:9, 18,20. and his retreat in Arabia in Gal. 1:17. and his return reformed. So some attempts to offer the existence of God even with our reasoning of Faith, may meet with failure.

10. The cultured despisers of Religion are suspicious of immature religion attacking "what" we claim by quoting their knowledge. However a mature believer understands HOW a God experience is a compelling Presence and an inner confidence helps a better seeing. It deals with an authentic Faith by people ability to deal with darkness, failure and non-validation of the Ego, and their quiet and confident joy. Infantile religion insists on "certitudes" every step of the way and thus not very happy.

11. Across the Universe a small remnant that knows this. No religion or lifestyle has a monopoly. Even Paul's fruits of the Spirit in Gal.5:22 that can be found across the boundaries of culture and religion. If not, it is indeed "a field of dry bones" Ezk.37 and very little new or good will happen there.

12. Jesus praises faith even more than love. "Your faith has saved you" Lk.8:48 Why? Because Faith is a 'breaking through' which allows us to hold on in the darkness as Jesus said in JN.1:5 "a light now shines in the darkness and the darkness cannot overpower it" without exception those who have found this deeper meaning of Faith, are those who have

suffered much or loved deeply. Because love and suffering are available to all as the eyes of true Faith.

Fear and Avoidance.

Fear has its roots in each person's perception of evil which is linked to our values, experience, sensitivities, imagination and fear of the unknown. This can cripple the ability to think rationally. It is a powerful force that can improve our safety or destroy our well being depending on what we let it do to us. When EXTERNAL avoidance is destructive, disciplined avoidance is sound for survival and growth. Sometimes to avoid what is expected to be unpleasant, can form a barrier to good experiences and a higher level of development. INTERNAL avoidance of handling fear is to seek to reduce our sensitivity, and this can cut off good and bad experiences. Psychological walls just like physical ones are both a means of protection and isolation. Likewise all sensitivities whether physical or emotional, play a vital part in preserving our well being. There is also a sense of a gift of fear, the power of Intuition our gut instincts that can protect us from danger or violence. A sense of fear, anxiety doubt or suspicion can on occasions save your life because it is believed intuition is usually correct. Teaching us that all felt and sensed communication is meaningful, to be listened to even if occasionally it is not urgent. These signals with an open mind we learn to educate our self. The "quiet small voice" which I have previously mentioned often describes a message or signal from the heart/gut brains is a powerful part of intuition which I have nurtured and found helpful in my life. Often dreams from R.E.M. "rapid eye movement" and R.G.M. "rapid gut movement" can send messages of physical problems or disease.

The fundamental message of Scripture is that God loves us and can be trusted JN.20:22-23 the non violent God whose very breath is identified with forgiveness. MATT.25:46.God is portrayed as violent, unloving and untrustworthy {these types of passages do not appear in other Gospels}. Why in Matthew and not in the others? Basically, because Matthew's Jewish Community was doing to the

Pharisees what they were doing to them. In Rome 70AD the Pharisees believed God was punishing them for allowing Jewish followers of Jesus to worship in their Synagogues and then say prayers for the Jewish followers of Jesus to perish. Then Matthew's community retaliated with prayers in their Christian Scripture for God to send the Pharisees to hell, MTT.23: 15-33, this passage is considered to be added by Matthew NOT Jesus saying. Jesus' message was one of unconditional LOVE. When they all forsake Jesus, the risen Christ rather than punishing them says He will be with them to the end of the age. Mtt.28: 20 and in LUKE "Father, forgive them for they do not know what they are doing" LK.23:34. In Mark no punishment. In JOHN 21:9-12 Jesus appears to His Apostles by the Sea of Galilee for breakfast. So for me Matthew sounds quite revengeful to the Pharisees harsh judgment of MATT.25:46 is one we bring upon ourselves. When we deny our true SOUL –LOVE [Life of valuable energy] our compassion and then ignore those in need we feel like "hell", thus God wants to restore us and bring us healing in God's Time.

Another difficult Scripture is 1Peter 3-19ff. It is not a literal trip by Jesus to a geographical place, but it is Jesus' utter merciful compassion for sinners whom Jesus identifies with completely at the point of dying on the cross. "My God, My God, why have you forsaken me?" MATT. 27:46 Jesus experiences the "hell" of God's absence. On occasions we need to check the translation as in MATT.5:43-48 it has been noted that there is no word in Aramaic for "perfect" and Jesus only, spoke in Aramaic, and could not have used the word "perfect". Matthew used the word "teleios" referring to a geometric term for perfect sculpture. So it is clear that Jesus was not asking us to be "perfect" in the sense of never making a mistake, but to forgive those who make mistakes as God does. The parallel passage in Luke 6:36 does not use the word "perfect", instead says, "be compassionate as your Father is compassionate" in the New Jerusalem Bible and the N.I.V. uses the word "merciful" Thus for judging all our Scripture interpretations MATT 22: 34-40 may help. So Jesus includes the Sadducees as well as the Pharisees with their Law and Scriptures, and included the Law as long as it was consistent with LOVE [life of valuable energy].

The Bible is not inerrant scientifically, historically or morally. Richard Rohr says the Bible is not about morality but about ONTOLOGY, which is about our "Being" who we are as daughters and sons of God. It is God's Love that saves us and God's authentic Life Of Valuable Energy is never vengeful, nor condemning and will always reach out to offer healing. When the Temple was cleansed MARK.11:17 it is proclaimed as a House of Prayer for all the Nations---not a place of sacrifice for Jews.

For Divorce Jesus went back to Genesis 1 and 2, rather than Moses Law.

Lk.16:18 and Mk.10:11.and Paul in 1Cor.7:10-16 and Matt. 5:32 / 19:9 preferred to follow Jesus Spirit of Love. For eating Jesus chose to eat with everyone as the way of sharing His LOVE, [life of valuable energy]. Jesus taught that the Scriptures [Old Testament] should be what was most compassionate, not necessarily the written word. Satan tempted Jesus in the wilderness by quoting the Scriptures. Jesus encourages us that our Scripture should result in growth of compassion and care for God, others, ourselves, and the world.

Then we have Palm Sunday and the branches were used to remind people of when Judas Macabues and his fighters took back the Temple from the Syrian oppressor Antiochus II with singing, palms and flag waving was blessing the war. So when people welcomed Jesus with palms they were communicating their desire for Jesus to lead a revolt against the Roman occupation. Instead Jesus chose to ride a lowly donkey and the Gospel of John 12:12-19 reports the people disappointment. This was Jesus' refusal to change power with anger and war. Jesus did challenge every dominating system of his time, and chose conscientious objection through non-violence. His disciples understood his message, so the following difficult passages should be understood in this light.

Before getting on the donkey, Jesus told this parable of the Pounds LK.19:11-27, often identified with the Parable of the Talents in MATT. 25:14-30. after reading these passages ask your self two questions. Which servant is the hero? Do you like the nobleman? However most Christians have heard a sermon emphasized our gifts or talents to be used well and God will reward us. This interpretation says God is no better than the nobleman who reinforces our cultural values, says the poor are lazy and wealth is God's Blessing. Presenting God as less caring and encouraging the use of USURY, this is far from the meaning Jesus intended. The Jews used Usury for investment of money and Jesus denounced this method as it denied Civil and Religious rights. The Jerusalem Bible footnote for this passage suggests Archelaus was probably the cruel nobleman Jesus referred to, as in 4 B.C. Herod the Great died. His son Archelaus went to Rome to receive his inheritance and was crowned King of Judea, and on his return murdered many people who did not like him.

We have to understand the context and the History of the time Jesus lived, to find the deeper meaning to His parables. As we know Jesus was also murdered by the system He consistently resisted. In Matt.2:22 Mary and Joseph are warned in a dream, not to return from Egypt to Archelaus's Judean Territory. This then seems the man who did not invest his money to support Archelaus Territory is the hero. Archelaus committed so many atrocities that Caesar Augustus deposed him in 6 A.D. for fear the Jews would riot. If this interpretation is correct, the parable is saying stand up and resist abusive systems at all costs. The Roman Empire's terror on the Cross became the Symbol of Faith for Christians, as Jesus Christ's Resurrection proclaimed that anger and violence does not have the last word. This clearly indicates WHY Jesus spoke in parables and metaphors.

This next parable is also often misunderstood because of the culture at the time of Jesus, this passage is Matt.5: 38-42. So knowledge of the History of the people at the time that Jesus spoke is all important for us to understand the meaning behind this parable. When we ask why Jesus said the "right cheek" we need to know Jesus' listeners knew the LEFT hand was unclean, and if they were to hit the LEFT cheek they would have to use their RIGHT hand, which would have to be the back of their hand. The back of the hand had special cultural meaning. The only people who could hit with the back of their hand were men with more power to give a backhander to people with less power. For instance, masters could backhand slaves, Romans could backhand Jews, husbands could backhand wives and parents would backhand their children and slaves who had no power. This purpose was to humiliate not physically hurt them. It was a social and emotional violence. So an equal would turn their LEFT cheek saying I am not beneath you and you cannot humiliate me. A cultural and creative way to avoid violence, Jesus is saying we should not suffer abuse nor should we cause abuse. Jesus encourages us to find a more creative way to solve problems and avoid all types of violence.

In the parable in Matt.5:38-42 and Lk.6:31-36 in the section about being sued for your coat and give your cloak as well. This was to do with an exploitive economic system where the Romans were taxing the Jews. It forced the poor to take out loans to pay their taxes and then to force the poor to default on the loans, so the rich could seize their land. Sometimes a man in debt would give collateral [a cow or some possession]. When the debtor had nothing left, the creditor would demand the debtor's outer garment. For the Jews this was common practice as noted in Exodus 22:25-27. This was a symbol of oppression in Jesus time, and to-day the saying, "taking the shirt off his back" is as degrading. So giving away your under garment meant then as now the person would be naked. In Jesus' culture it was not so scandalous to be naked, as it was for another person to experience the humiliation he received by having to look at a naked man. It brought home how his treatment of the debtor made the creditor appear, a situation that degrades all of us. Jesus taught this to those who would listen, to find a solution without violence, and hopefully for the oppressor to repent. Then to go the second mile was to do with the Roman law at the time in Palestine. This required a Roman soldier could require a civilian to carry their packs which weighed 60-80 pounds for one mile, if he demanded more he could be punished. So when they came to the marker on the road, Jesus suggested they keep carrying the pack, which meant the soldier had to plead to have the pack returned to him, incase he was caught and punished. Again Jesus teaches us to regain our dignity and exercise our power to refuse to be a victim, without getting caught up in a violent situation. To create a nonviolent way to resist, when He says " resist an evil doer", having given three examples of oppression and abuse in His time. We are not to be passive victims, as Jesus encourages us to find creative non-violent ways to resist, as best we can under the circumstances, by speaking the truth even if taking us to the Cross, because this passage has commonly been interpreted to be tolerant of abuse.

Matt.5:38-42 is an excellent example of how difficult it is to understand Scripture in a loving way when we do not understand the context of the time when Jesus was living. This teaches us we should not interpret Scripture that encourages abuse of us or others. This goes against Jesus' LOVE [Life of Valued Energy] that He gives to all humans at our birth His will and desire, as LOVE is not a feeling, this is the same for us. The Bible is a process of growth and development of our understanding of the nature of God and His LOVE in which violence and self-interest diminish, and compassion and care for each other and the community increases. This can be seen where only white men had "rights" in the world to an increasing dignity of value of all human cultures. From a legalistic image of God to a compassionate, forgiving and healing God.

Richard Rohr reminds us the Old Testament used the Dueteronomic Code 24:10-13-17, led them to expect punishment rather than healing for unrepentant sinners as in the case of the Egyptian plagues. Then we have Jesus on the Cross saying "Father forgive them, they know not what they do," as God offers FORGIVENESS for sinners. Then Matt. 22:34-40 gives us Jesus answering the Pharisees, with what is normal interpretation for all Scripture from Deuteronomy 6:5. Several Theologians point out that many Jews wanted the Messiah to be vengeful to the Romans and Syrians but Jesus omitted the passage in Isaiah 61:2 and declared Gods favour rested on all " the just and the unjust", Jesus proclaimed an end to violent punishment of ones enemies. This was going against literalistic interpretation of Scripture and Jesus was often inviting the people to grow beyond this as He healed on the Sabbath or touched a leper or forgave those who asked Him. An example was the adulterous woman John 8:2-12 who the

Scribes and Pharisees wanted stoned to death, the Law of Moses in Deut.22:20 and Leviticus 20:10 Jesus was disliked for setting aside this punishment passage for a more compassionate understanding of the WILL of God. This move from the Old Testament Purity Laws in Lev.11:44 and Lev.17-26 also Exodus 33:19. to Compassion in Isaiah 58:1-12 then to a capacity to Love unconditionally in Matt.5:44-45 which means Gods Life of Valuable Energy in all He has Created. Jesus was teaching that God was not continuing the destruction of enemy groups as they previously believed was the Will of YAHWEH, in the Law of Moses. Josh 11:14-15.

This was a struggle for the early Christian Church as it still is for many people to-day. This stems from Church laws misunderstanding Jesus' deeper message that God wanted to fulfill what the Prophets had been teaching in the Scriptures and had been killed. They did not comprehend God's unconditional compassion and went on to also kill Jesus. We are living with far greater study of culture, language and meanings to-day, and can be open to the deep psychological depth in the Parables, Stories and Metaphors that Jesus told. The people were experiencing through His words, miracles and healing, compared to the Scribes and Pharisees who were mainly quoting literal Scripture to try and trap Him and accusing Him of denying the Scriptures. The Old Testament was written by Scribes, leaders, teachers and the prophets of HOW the people experienced God over the Ages, moving away from God and moving back to God, in a rhythm trying to follow and to worship Him. To-day several Theologians have discovered that the Gospel of Matthew has three different authors and very different attitudes, who wrote approximately 20—40 years apart. The early author believed the letter of the Purity Law and they were the only ones saved. The other authors are commonly known as the Q Tradition and Marks Gospel. The final Matthew writes with the compassion of Jesus. So all the Gospel writers attempt to portray Jesus as they experienced his values, compassion, healing and social needs of the poor, the children, women and the diseased. They remembered his parables and stories of how to live life putting God first, neighbours and then ourselves. Recognising the Spirit of God in us to care for, and guide others in service and in health the appropriate and compassionate way. The Theologians date early Matthew at 30-60 A.D. and final Matthew 80-85 A.D. These Gospels were possibly written by sacred men who wanted the stories collected by word of mouth or writings gathered as their recognition of GOD in the human form of JESUS. Thus was formed their new inclusive relationship in the Eucharist, the Blood of Jesus. Matt. 26:28. As the New Testament grew also the new direction of Universal Compassion grew.

In 49 A.D. there was a struggle between the two factions in the early Christian Church and the Council of Jerusalem met. ACTS.15:4-29. The division was between the Circumcision Party, the Jewish Christians who wanted the pagans to keep the Law of Moses ACTS. 15:5, and the Gentile Christians led by Paul, who wanted freedom from the "ritual laws" that they felt were not following the compassionate way of Jesus, by giving them the Holy Spirit. This was supported by Peter. To-day we can see a modern struggle between fundamentalism and the Catholic view of Scripture [catholic meaning Universal Christianity not a particular church] and literalistic interpretation by the law. Jesus was born under the law we read in GAL.4:4 but was teaching LOVE [life of valued energy] was more important than the law [to value the life of people.] Thus it was established that through Jesus God longs for the salvation of all people. The Catholic approach is grounded in the understanding that the Gospels and Letters were written between 40-60 years after the death and Resurrection of Christ. Also a large percentage of Theologians acknowledge that none of the writers were eye witnesses of what Jesus said and did, as their information came from various communities. Many authors are limited by from whom they receive their material, as well as culture personalities, education and experience of God in their lives. All of this accounts for some contradictory statements in the Bible such as Matt.10:5 where Jesus tells the 12 Apostles "to go nowhere among the Gentiles" whereas in Matt.28:19 Jesus says "go therefore to make disciples of all nations". This helps us understand what the Jerusalem Council did all those years ago, that the Bible is not a rule of life, but a journey with God.

Biblical Fundamentalism tries to find direct answers for living through the Bible. The Bible is not intended to provide ready made answers for unforeseeable Theological and Moral issues that would arise in following centuries. Life of Valuable Energy [love], that is what God's Creation is and it is Revelation. It affirms that God dwells within each person and in all of life in a non-violent and life giving way for those who work with God. There are times of wars and cruelty when evil raises its head. Our experience is that Revelation is not over, as God is constantly revealing Himself to us in powerful ways. At first they called Jesus a Prophet, but Jesus changed that Authority to Himself, by the way He taught His parables and stories. Jesus makes it clear in the Gospel of John," He is the Way, the Truth and the Life," by showing how God is always revealing Himself to us in everyday life and to trust our own experience, to find revelation in nature and all creatures great and small. This is advanced Prayer at the Heart of all Creation. This is called universal consciousness and Teilhard de Chadin called this consciousness the LOVE [Life of Valued Energy] of God. I believe I was very Blessed to have three wonderful Christian Mentors who developed my potential and character. You can find Mentors who you can trust to help transform your life when you are experiencing struggle, do not hesitate as you deserve to honour your life of valuable energy.

It is written that Science is consistently increasing their findings with the Bible, to agree that God dwells within all of life. To get in touch with what leads us to Faith, Hope and Love. You may well ask what does Love mean? It means it is God's Gift at our birth   of--:L—LIFE—O—OF—V—VALUABLE---E---ENERGY, with the Gift of Freedom which has a partner called Discipline. As previously stated LOVE is not a feeling, it is a decision of our Will we make to care for others, sometimes with compassionate feelings. As humans we are part of God's Creation and with our Love and disciplined Freedom we are to be of service to others, especially to the young and vulnerable so they learn to grow up to understand their purpose and meaning in life of Valued Energy. There is another word called Consolation that makes us more connected to ourselves, to others, God and nature. So we move away from the

71

root word "FEAR"[feeling, ,envy ,anger, revenge] all the negative words we use stem from the word Fear that disconnect us from God, our families and relationships in life. When we move away from fear and negative thinking, we find there is "nothing as strong as gentleness and nothing as gentle as real strength". In the Bible Peace is a word to encourage people to enrich and care for each other in Love which I believe means their Life of Valuable Energy which is where we place our desire. Jesus' peace in John14:27 and Jn.16:33 is inner peace in our heart.

Generally the Biblical sense of peace has the meaning of the Hebrew word SHALOM , which expresses the ideal state of life in Israel. Translated as harmony and peace is free growth of the Soul and harmonious community. Peace is central to the preaching of the Old Testament prophets, then salvation with righteousness and truth. The Suffering Servant brings Peace to the Nations in Isaiah 53:5. The long awaited gift of the last days in Romans 2:10 which was to bring deliverance from the enemies and the promise of righteousness. This was first with the birth of John the Baptist Luke2:29-30 and then with Jesus the coming of the Kingdom of God hoped for by the Disciples Luke 19:44 but rejected by the Nation. The New Testament brings out the meaning of Peace being those who make peace between warring parties reproduce the character of God Matthew 5:9 and so the same should happen between the disciples Mark 9:50. The miracles are signs of the Kingdom in creating, healing and peace and removing fear and disorder Mark 5:34 and John 7:23. This supreme gift of peace that Jesus brings is different from worldly security John 14:27 as we should understand that even to-day. This means the Life, Death and Resurrection of Jesus Christ can be called God's Gospel of Peace as Jesus passes on this message for us to do the same. Peace is also part of Eternal life which produces Freedom and a Life of Valuable Energy 1Corinthians 7:15 and Colossians 3:15. Peace is to be the Spiritual Unity of the life of the church Ephesians 4:3 to be pursued and maintained in faith and discipline in face of foolish arguments or jealousy 2 Timothy 2:22-23 in worldly wisdom in contrast to heavenly wisdom.

Chapter 9

DISCOVERING OUR ETERNAL TRUE SOUL

John 3: 16. John 17:3 Matthew 16:26.

E.T.E.R.N.A.L. Experience True Effort
Reality Natural And Learned

What is our true Soul? In my research we usually learn we have a Soul some where in our teens. By then we will have understood we have a Body, Mind and Spirit. These together are who we are as a human being and known as our Soul, so to speak our spiritual engine that drives us. Soul refers to the immortal or spiritual part of a person, the moral or emotional nature and the spiritual or emotional warmth of humans. It is considered the essential part of quality or principle of a person, and also considered the Spirit of a dead person separate from the body, having an existence of its own. To discover our true Soul means we are required to do self-discovery [or seek psychological help] often called self-assessment, to find our deeper feelings and emotions from the treatment we have experienced. How we react or respond to all our experience good or bad, helpful or unhelpful. This is how we are going to cope and be honest with ourselves before we can be honest with other human beings, and creatures great and small. It is essential to understand our true Soul to reach a level of happiness we want for life. When we have had a disadvantaged up bringing, we may have to unlearn some unhelpful habits and attitudes, and also learn forgiveness of our self and others. This is hard work but worth the effort for a peaceful life. Life is full of effort, so give your self gentle strength treatment and find God's help which is available and possible.

Our Soul is often called our Identity or True Self /False Self [means inadequate] We are all unique human beings who are not the same as our parents, relations or siblings. Thus our feelings and emotions are ours and we need to own all of them, good and not so good. With effort we can change or control the not so good feelings that are of the negative kind, such as frustration, irritation, fear, evil anger, revenge, denial, depression or suicide. I call this the Dawn of Awareness that opens up options and power of choices, when we put Freedom and Power together we get joy. Be aware of something we are fearful is coming from, may be from our childhood. There is a certain amount of scariness in everything in life birth, commitment, marriage, jobs and death. At times we can get stuck and paralized with fear, we then need to change our negative emotional response to a positive response. Anger is a normal emotion, like any other e-motion [energy in motion] what we do with it is good or evil, moral or immoral. Anger can be used for good and turned into helpful channels. Sadly some people bottle it up in their bodies, which may be anger from their past. Be yourself and do not displace anger, which means taking it out on yourself when you are angry with some one else.

Finding our Identity

Many people, women and men think to find a sense of Identity is difficult to achieve. My first answer to that is laziness, sadly a favorite choice of those who do not want to make an effort, or their own self-development. To search for our true identity is essentially the truth of meaning and purpose in our lives, how we relate to the world around us. We may well ask where does our search begin? Many people move from one Church to another or another Religion, or to Science or their own health achievements. Often not one single perspective reveals the truth. There is a need of Balance of Physical health, Mental attitudes and Faith [body, mind and spirit]. As any job we do requires effort, so we have to apply effort to discover our conscious and sub- conscious emotions. These feelings of fear, dislikes, negative experiences and how we accept criticism, also the joys and kindness we enjoy and learning as we mature and grow. It has been called our True Self and our False Self [meaning inadequate]. We need to observe and discover what hurts us mentally and spiritually, as well as our physical being, and why it disturbs us or scares us. It may come from our childhood influence or a later bad experience that undermines our confidence and courage. So getting our 3 Brains in balance with each other [Body—Heart—Mind—Head---Spirit---Feelings] helps our decision making in a more calm and peaceful way. Knowing ourselves in all aspects of our Being takes us to a higher relaxed level of understanding and response with a contented happiness we all aim to achieve. Especially if we receive unexpected mental, verbal or physical abuse, we can recognize it is the other persons problem and calmly handle it.

A helpful place to start looking for our True Soul [identity] is asking our self in which order of these 5 Love Languages are most meaningful to us.

1. Words of Affirmation.
2. Quality Time.
3. Receiving Gifts.
4. Acts of Service.
5. Physical Touch.

These five love languages all relate to us as small children, as parents we are often unaware of their use for life until we become aware of our need to learn our future partners love language. There is a great need for these love language messages to be observed and recognized in small children. When these messages are neglected it may lead to rebellion and become bullies or violence in their teens, as a child may feel unloved because their emotional needs have not been met. These love messages are valuable tools to train our children and for men and women to enjoy better relationships. We must not expect Governments to do the job for us. They are not voted in to teach us how to value and nurture our children. All parents are responsible for how our children grow up physically, mentally, emotionally and spiritually.

WORDS OF AFFIRMATION

These are words of encouragement these require empathy to see the world from your child or your spouses perspective. What holds us back is often confidence, we must use kind words to communicate. A Sage once said "a soft answer turns away anger" and forgiveness is love and value which makes requests not demands.

QUALITY TIME

This is giving some one our undivided attention, listening for feelings and observing body language. Sharing events that happened that day, and quality shared activities and interests.

RECEIVING GIFTS

Gifts are symbols of love like wedding rings. They are an outward and visible sign of an inward and spiritual Grace that unites two hearts. Symbols have emotional value. The gift of presence, being there when our spouse needs us or in a time of crisis and do not expect him/her to read your mind.

ACTS OF SERVICE

This is doing things your spouse would like you to do with a positive spirit. Our acts of service are often modeled by our parents or by our own personality. Be aware acts of service are not done out of fear, guilt or resentment.

PHYSICAL TOUCH

This is a way of communicating emotional love [valuable life energy]. Love touches may be Explicit and demand full attention as in marriage. Love touches may be Implicit, a simple touch on a hand or shoulder. Learn how to make decisions without destroying unity. Find your partner's love message, and how to speak each others love message. Jesus said "Give and it will be given to you". Mother Teresa said "We can do no great things, we can only do small things with great love". God's total commitment to Love brings a total commitment to Freedom. My Acronym brings Life Of Valuable Energy For Responsible Energized Eternal Discipline Of Mind, which means God gave up enforcement and control. God is clearly not a Policeman. No other way for God to act because God is Love itself. 1John 4:8, 16, 18. Divine Compassion and Mercy in one direction, and an ever more creative life and love that is stronger than death. This is the True Soul we are seeking to discover. Grace is who God is, Grace is everywhere and we can enjoy unearned love in our self and allow it in everyone else. I believe God gives us our Soul and deepest Identity our True Self. We do not make or create our Soul, we just grow it up. 1Cor.12:10 Paul's wisdom of discerning Spirits.

The Picanniny Dawn of Awareness.

Through my expansive window pane
came a searching light to frame,
The tumbling silver lining clouds
weaving threads of deepening gold.

Through the crooked limbs and sticks
of eucalyptus leaves and trees,
Introducing the rising baby dawn
like a dancing diamond in the sky.

Then the glassy horizon eclipses
The expanding, galloping shades
Of fiery reds, gold and azure blue,
to highlight the frangipani tree.

Which the early birds are feasting on
to encourage their young to fly free.
God's gentle breathe among the leaves.
Not just yet no early morning breeze.

How emerging faith leads us gaze upon
Creation's divine dance come to ease,
Searching hearts and souls to embrace
Picanniny dawns awaking Holy Grace.

Contemplative seeing, thinking, praying with the Holy Spirit.

JOHN 19:30 JN 20:21-23 JN3:8 Divine wind blows where it wills, and breathes on us forgiveness. The air we breath is the same air that all humans, nature and creatures great and small breath, and it cannot be controlled as the Spirit wills it so. I wrote this poem the morning after the Blood Moon the night before, when waking and found my contemplative prayer being taken over when seeing this dawn.

1. The light rising out of darkness.

2. Nature's beauty breaking out with awe and wonder.

3. To see God's breath stirring life with gentle Spirit ease.

This is my deep, deep silent experience of God's presence in my life. It has been written by others there are three ways of seeing.

1. The physical eye of the flesh that touches, moves and sees beauty, enjoys.

2. The eye of reason, meditation and reflection.

3. The eye of true understanding when all head heart and gut are in unity is called mystery contemplation, the contemplative gaze of awe and wonder. My experience when writing the poem of the dawn of awareness we read in 1 Corinthians 2:9-11. Several of the early Mystics have said the loss of these Eyes in our Western world religion and Spirituality shows the difficulty that Governments and Leaders have to move from the Ego desire for control and dualistic thinking with lack of Wisdom and Vision. The True Mystic contemplative person is both humble and compassionate as they do not know "certainty" of God's final Mystery. A Mystic is one who has moved from a mere thinking belief system to actual inner experience, that Jesus is calling us to in John 10:19-

38 and we can only lead people as far as we have gone in our experience. I can only persuade you to follow Jesus wonderful teaching.

This is considered to be opposite dualistic thinking, meaning dying to self importance. I have for some years sought to develop a non-dualistic approach to vision of our future for life and community in which we live. This vision I have encompasses JOHN 10:19-38 and I believe is desirable and available to everyone. I have read it is what the Mystics explain as actual inner experience as different from just having a belief system. Also Paul in 2Cor.12:2-4. All of which means a true search for meaning of a God who creates human life, nature and all creatures great and small that keep creating themselves, with Divine guidance.

The early years of desire to discover myself and to access "why and how" I accepted, rather than reacted to criticism or correction from my teachers and Grandmother [having lost my Mother]. I did not make many judgments or blame others. I believe this was because my Mother did not treat me or other people that way. Neither did the wonderful teachers at Kambala who helped develop my character from age 7. I was voted class captain 8 out of my 10 years, some tennis and netball teams and a prefect of the school the year before leaving school. I was told by a teacher that I was popular because I did not criticize or blame my school mates. I can only relate that to how I was treated as a small child. That is my reason today to endeavour to lead others to a well balanced attitude and gentle strength which is creative energy and shared power, I experienced while growing up. My experience from my father and first husband was the opposite. They were control freaks and I am sure they were brought up by fathers who controlled and punished them as role models of how with anger and selfish attitudes to treat women and children. My father's treatment of me was after I left school and after canceling my application to do nursing, made sure I had no money and forced me into a marriage to a man with whom I had not had a conversation and he had not even asked me to marry him and told my father he had and my father would not listen to me. They both considered it their right to treat me according to their will, they did not want forgiveness. Some years ago Jesus taught me I could forgive them and find healing, which I certainly have found with guidance from the Holy Spirit. This is forgiveness through Contemplative Prayer.

This is my reason to write to hopefully encourage women to help guide men who are fathers, to have gentle strength and shared control when teaching and training their sons in their maleness, I believe females cannot train boys to be males. This is essential for mental, physical and spiritual health, to prevent confusion in their teens as they mature to adulthood. I believe Angry Controlling Strength is self –destructive as well as hurting other people. Gentle Strength is not a weakness it is well balanced self-controlled creative energy and power. Fathers who show this are living a role model of Love [Life Of Valuable Energy].

Dualistic Thinking

Some understanding about dualistic thinking, it is knowing most things by comparison. Once we have compared things or labeled them [judge them] we almost always conclude, one is good and the other is bad or less good / for me or against me / right or wrong / black or white. This is why "stinking thinking" of racism, sexism, homophobia and prejudice of all kinds are hard to overcome, and lasted so long even among nice people. A dualistic mind compares, competes, conflicts, conspires, condemns and cancels out any contrary evidence and then crucifies with impunity. It is often called the 7 C's of delusion and the source of most violence. Sadly very few Christians have been taught how to live with LAW and FREEDOM at the same time, which limits our thinking for holding a creative tension when required. Jesus through His stories and parables counter punches the dualistic thinking, with a non-dualistic language, commonly known today as a contemplative approach to understanding. The Doctrine of the Trinity was made in order to defeat the dualistic mind and invite us into non-dualistic, holistic consciousness. I have read where the world of science, biology and astrophysics is now affirming this Trinitarian truth from very different angles. These disciplines see that all of creation is in relationship. All is a constant changing of forms through a non stop process of loss and renewal, death and resurrection, losing the false self and finding the true self.

Richard Rohr gives us a teaching tool that maybe helpful for some people, to understand Dualistic thinking.

1. My body and self image is who I am.

2. My external behaviour is who I am. I need to look good on the outside and hide from myself my unbalanced parts.

3. My thoughts and feelings are who I am. To have better thoughts and feelings and then control them and do not see them in myself. This is considered our shadow character. To move on, a shock or humiliation usually is suffered to go beyond this stage.

4. Deeper felt knowledge in my body is who I am. This discovery is very informative and helpful but some people get stuck there in dismay.

5. My shadow self is who I am my weakness comes to overwhelm me. Without Grace, guidance and prayer often return to previous identities. Need to give self time in silent prayer and search out guidance.

6. I am empty and powerless, any attempts to save self does not work. What we need to do is wait, trust and prayer to discover and learn faith. God will soon become real often in hindsight.

7. I am much more than who I thought I was. Death of the false self, and birth of the true self, which may feel like a gentle void.

8. "I and the Father are one" John 10: 30. we find God is in us and we are in God. When this is known we do not have to prove it to anyone.

9. I am who I am, just me warts and all just human. No need to be anything other than I am living in God's image of me, both the good and the bad. This experience when completed is moving us deeper into Faith knowing we will receive guidance from God.

Non-Dualistic Thinking

A non-dualistic way of thinking is now considered a Contemplative approach to thinking, for a more calm and peaceful approach. This can take a number of years' experience of conflict, confusion, healing and forgiving reality in life. This is a capacity to value the negative life experiences into a positive healing we call Salvation. This calm approach allows us to confront the negative with greater clarity, courage and action with God's help. Contemplative thinking is when our Heart Brain grows larger as we move towards the realization that One God creates all and values all. To get there we need honest self-observation and a creative tension between Law and Freedom, a paradox necessary for Spiritual growth. Matt.7:21-29 and in Romans and Galations. Life is hard and we are our own worst enemy when we deny this, before the Truth sets us free, it tends to make us miserable. Some people call this "the family crab bucket" because it is hard to get out when all the other crabs are pulling us back". I believe God gives us our Soul, and deepest identity, our true self. We do not make or create our Soul we just grow it up. This is Paul's wisdom that he calls discerning Spirits 1Cor.12:10.

It is helpful to remember not to eliminate negative life experiences but turn them into a positive when possible. A quick example: "a miner in the goldfields saw my car had a flat tyre and when I came out of the shop said, "I can't wait to see a liberated woman change a tyre and I replied, 'Jack I am so liberated I can ask you to do it for me please,' he burst out laughing and said 'I did not expect that answer, yes I will do it for you', and he did." I do not believe I have to prove I can do what men can do better and quicker. Contemplative thinking does not eliminate negative language and rejects the idea "that does not make sense". It sharpens our rational mind and increases the ability to see the humble truth without our fears in the way. Paul in 1Cor.13:12. There is no moral outrage of contradictions and mystery. It allows us to practice compassion, mercy, kindness, patience, forgiveness and humility. Too often we are taught to be judgmental of others to look for mistakes and failure in ourselves and others and to miss the message or to project it on to others.

Perhaps this is what Jesus is telling us in Matthew.7:3 to "see the splinter in our neighbour eye, while unable to see the plank in our own eye". Then in James 1:8"a person in two minds will be unstable in all they do". In Rom.12:2 Paul says we need a new balanced mind [heart, head, gut coherence] of how we hear and pass on our experiences. We need a new mind says Paul in Eph.4:23-24 "we need the mind of Christ" 1Cor.2:16 a Spiritual growth. We need a contemplative approach to thinking more peaceful and calm which may take a number of years experience of conflict, healing and forgiving reality in life. This non-dualistic thinking has the capacity to learn to love [value] the negative life experiences into a positive healing that we call Salvation. This calm attitude allows us to confront the negative with greater clarity with Gods help. Non-dualistic contemplative thinking is when our Heart Brain grows larger and we realize that God creates all and values all. When we want to get there we need some honest self-observation to grow our Spirit. This involves a creative tension between Law and Freedom Matt.7:21-29 also in Romans and Galations.

Others have suggested to try these questions to exercise the mind:

THINK

1. T.---is it true?

2. H.---is it helpful?

3. I. ---is it inspiring?

4. N.---is it necessary?

5. K.---is it kind

What is the meaning of Spiritual Love / Value. I have understood for about 50 years that Jesus was / is the supreme psychologist the world has ever known. This He physically demonstrated with miracles, and spoke about in stories, parables and metaphors, in the local Aramaic language to help those to benefit, who did not have the higher education. This was to encourage the people and us to see, not only with our eyes, but also with our heart, head and gut feelings to love / value God first, then ourselves and others of all cultures, the diseased and disabled children and women. He did this with compassion, kindness, gentle strength and God's Grace with faith. As previously mentioned I have endeavored to unpack the word LOVE, which is a gift along with freedom given by God at our birth. I believe the meaning of the word Love is "Life Of Valuable Energy" some call an "Acronym". This gift is for us to learn how to apply this valuable energy in our life. This early blossoming of our Spirit is gradually developed as we grow to responsible adulthood.

This means discovering our Identity of confidence, courage, creativity, and how we want to communicate and be committed. This means being awake and aware of the changes of our life cycle and humanity of all the people who touch our life.

To learn our conscious and sub-conscious thoughts with our physical, mental and emotional changes that toss our feelings and actions about in life. Such as Jesus' teaching in Luke.9:24 "losing one self to find oneself". This is opening up our heart and soul to a deeper meaning of our identity in finding our true freedom with its partner called Discipline. This is a gradual awareness of our whole being, finding our seeing, hearing, touching and breathing senses leading to a deep peace and contentment. "This Spiritual love / energy will teach you all things and remind you of all that I have taught you" Jesus said in John14:26.

In my childhood the Bush Brotherhood [Anglican Church] Priests came and lived in our house for 3 months of every year, until my Mother died when I was 10 years old. My Father owned a large sheep station in South West Queensland on the Maranoa River between Mitchell and St. George. The Priest would take Church services on our lawn for various families in a 30 mile radius of the property for one month. Then move on by the Mail Truck or by another station owner and return again during the year. It was my Mother who taught me to love God as much as I loved her, and that God loved me very much. When children are raised with that teaching and application as we grow up, it makes learning the meaning of Spiritual Love real. I also learnt that if God and my mother loved me, I can love / value myself. That was a real base to my confidence, which helped me when I had to go to Boarding school in Sydney at age 7. When my Mother died having a baby I was 10 years old, and a wonderful school teacher Hilda Epstein told me Jesus would look after me if I trusted Him, and not to blame God, my Father, the Doctor anyone else, that we humans make our own problems and diseases.

Those early years grounded me for what life still throws at me. This is one reason why I want to try and help young women on their own or who have husbands or partners who are not giving enough attention to their children to encourage them to raise their children with gentle strength to give them confidence with a life of valuable energy. The boys need their fathers to give them the special understanding of their maleness as females cannot teach this to their sons. This is because boys think differently to girls, sisters and mothers and so girls think differently to boys. This is very important for boys to be nurtured by caring fathers from the cradle through their young years. So when they reach their teens they are not confused when their hormones kick in and change their feelings and desires. All children should be taught how valuable they are even when making mistakes, which are not wrong but learning experiences. This is valuable parenting for your sakes as well as the boys. I have buried 6 male suicides, I make my point. Then we can see other humans in the same way as being human and learning as we live a life of valuable energy. So we operate at the deepest level of consciousness with freedom and desire for happiness. They call this the glue that joins us humans together the gift of LOVE [Life Of Valuable Energy]. This is what we are created for, to then pass on the same to others. Some words of St. John of the Cross to remember "Love what God sees in You".

To discover our true self is to understand and accept paradox, which means grasping the truth of something that seems a contradiction. We must learn to live with paradox, because Reality is paradoxical. This means to be wise, forgiving and patient to form good relationships, as we are all mixed Blessings. There is always a mixture of good and bad, helpful and unhelpful and living and dying. Jesus is our role model of paradox,---human yet divine---physical yet spiritual male body and a female soul---killed yet lives---victim yet victor---failure yet redeemer---incarnate yet cosmic---nailed to a cross yet liberated. Jesus encourages us to see the same truth in ourselves and all creatures great and small. What is the purpose of living unless we are learning, and we are all learning together. When we acknowledge that the Holy Spirit of God is part of us, we can accept that the paradox of Jesus is also in us, and His calling us to imitate Him. In the past all the Mysteries were not connected, but we can now see the Cosmic Christ has reconciled them to Himself. We are now able to recognize these great paradoxes in ourselves. COL.1:15-20. This we can now see we have worshiped Jesus without following Him, thus putting Jesus on a pedestal above and separate and removed from us, instead of a journey toward a union with God. This is a move from just belonging to being transformed into Union with God, and enables us to hold together all the paradoxes we have like Christ, the one God of all Creation.

The work of discovering our identity, our true self is a life time experience. Confidence found, courage and creativity developed and gently guided in our childhood, through our teens and into early adulthood is a good base to start. This involves enjoying our learning in this life of valuable energy. When we are leaving home and entering the School of Life, we need to listen, not only from parents, and recognize help from our three Brains to be consistent and reliable. This starts with our Heart Brain which is compassion, values and kindness. Then pass the Heart message and feelings on to our Head Brain which is the creative process that generates new lines of thinking. Then back to the Heart Brain to balance these thoughts and feelings. Then on to the Gut Brain which is the courage and action component to keep us safe from harm and danger, to mobilize or immobilize into flight---fright---or freeze. This is the ability to act in the face of fear. Then back to the Heart Brain to operate when all three are balanced.

This comes from Grant Soosalu and Marvin Oka's book 'mBraining' which I have read and can be found on the Internet.

1. Compassion---kindness---values come from our Heart Brain.

2. Creativity---is the process we generate new ideas and direction from the Head Brain.

3. Courage is how to put decisions into action from the Gut Brain.

4. These three Brains must be balanced before putting into action then the outcomes work very well, when Compassion, Creativity and Courage are well aligned. This is about listening between the three Brains for communication, caring, consistency and competence. The Brains need to be able to trust the skill of awareness and knowledge of each other to perform their prime function.

There are 3 constraints for alignment:

1. One Brain is used to the exclusion of the others.

2. When one of the 3 Brains is in conflict with the others.

3. When the 3 Brains are working but used in the wrong sequence.

It is recommended that this sequence works best:---Heart—Head—Heart—Gut—Heart. Wisdom is the payoff for working to establish communication with our 3 Brains for decision making and taking the following action.

1. For setting goals and outcomes.

2. Decision making.

3. Problem solving.

4. Motivation.

5. Harnessing our intuition.

6. Cultivating understanding.

7. Personal learning and behaviour changes.

8. Relationships.

9. Health and well being.

How we raise our children from the cradle through their young years and teens is the main foundation for their well being and character to give them confidence, resilience and courage to learn their own skills and free choices. Boys need fathers with gentle strength to help them treat themselves and girls and women with valuable care and kindness to build relationships with a well balanced sense of shared gifts and energy, to be an honest creative role model. For girls and boys, men and women to learn to share their talents, time and energy in values, friendships, health marriages and business operations as they grow older to credit themselves and the world as well balanced happy humans.

It is important boys understand that they think and act differently to girls and the same for girls as they develop and treat each other with value and respect. This is essential learning very young to avoid suicide and domestic violence which is deep anger learned how they were treated when very young and stored in their sub-conscious and comes out when older. This lack of control when hidden causes horrific tragedies and very hard to change over 20 year of age. It becomes a complete lack of self value so no one else is of value, the supreme selfish act and a huge mental problem which I believe we parents have to fix.

Governments are not voted in to nurturer and value our children character and personalities with kindness and gentle strength and guidance for life. They can and do help with some health, education and work.

V.A.L.U.E. for me means Vision Aware Love Understands Empathy.

L.O.V.E. I believe is the Gift from God at our birth a Life Of Valuable Energy. What is Energy? I believe it is effort and sadly many do not want to make the effort. For us humans to have a Life of Value it takes Creative Energy to Love other lives. It is not a feeling it is our desire, our will to make a personal choice some times intimate valued connection with another human Being. May you find your puzzle pieces in your True Soul of compassionate consistent contentment.

Chapter 10

RECOGNISING WHERE GOD IS AND THE HOLY SPIRIT

Matthew 1: 22-23. John 14:9-21 John 20:21-23.
Romans 5:12-21. John 16:12-15.

**G.O.D. Goodness over Death. HOLY SPIRIT
Honour our Lord Yearly.**

Our limited knowledge of God is the Bible through the Old Testament and Jesus in the New Testament. Belief in the existence of God comes to us Christians, is how God revealed himself through Jesus Christ, showing God's love for all, humans, all creatures great and small and nature to give us Eternal Life. Jews, Muslims, Christians and other authentic religions all worship the one true God, and use different names from their cultures and stories from their Prophets. In the Bible we understand God as the Creator of everything, and with God all things are possible God as teacher, friend who is just and merciful, whose presence is everywhere in the form of Spirit. Who is goodness, truth and love, the Alpha and Omega [which means the beginning and the end]. In other religions they have many more words and phrases for God.

There has often been debate about whether God is alternative, personal or impersonal, unity or trinity, male or female, close or remote. As we often use the word 'or' perhaps we should use the word 'and' as He is all of these. In the New Testament and the Gospel of John 1:1-14, Jesus is referred to "THE WORD was with God and the word was God". In John 14:9-10 "who has seen me has seen the Father—the Father and I are one" and in Matthew 28:18-20 " go therefore and make disciples of all nations, Baptizing them in the name of the Father, the Son and the Holy Spirit". Despite our advanced science we have little understanding of many theories and debates that remain inconclusive.

So here we have our Mystery with God's work of Creation. To confirm or rule it out, as we only have theories to explain the existence of Natural Law being created from nothing. Thus Science explanation is a process of evolution, and the Bible indicates an act of design and teaches that every species was formed by an intelligent being from the resources of the earth to bare off spring according to its own kind. Then with natural change as well as creation and design working together, different races must surely be the outcome of a natural process from the first human beings and their descendants.

With some scientists Divine intervention is unacceptable. Perhaps a reaction to a God who runs everything in the Universe or to account for what they could not understand at the time, and is inadequate with the pace of discovery. These reactions exist when simplistic interpretations in the Bible such as "God made the universe in 6 days" when they overlook the Biblical quote "For the Lord the day is like a thousand years and a thousand years is like a day". As far as we know Jesus avoided discussing the laws of Nature. Jesus did not give models of reality of the time which may become obsolete in the future. This evidence in the Scriptures helps us understand the concept of God as both Unity and Trinity, as well as the components of evolution and the survival of the fittest which we can observe in plant and animal species.

In the Scriptures Old Testament and New Testament Christ made it clear we cannot save ourselves by every fine detail of the Law, but salvation comes through co-operation between us and God. Christ did not abolish what was written in the Old Testament, but came to fulfill the promises made by the Prophets for humans to enter the Kingdom of God. This Jesus explains in his messages, that the Spirit of the Law takes priority over the Letter of the Law. Plus the greatest two Commandments are the commitment to honor God first and then our neighbours and our self captured in Jesus words "the Sabbath was made for man, not man for the Sabbath". Here through Jesus teachings God comes closer rather than distant or remote, with an emphasis placed on friendship rather than on blood relationships. This change would come about, not through disagreements but through stages of development which humanity must pass to enter the Kingdom of God.

These rules and discipline should be taught by the parents or guardians to improve their children's prospects of survival and for their well being of their Soul/Spirit. Then as they mature and given more freedom with God's gift of Life of Valued Energy, and greater responsibility for themselves, with the understanding of where God is in Creation. The story of God's guidance for humanity lies in the responsible response of How, When and Where parents, family and friends lead the next generations to the Truth and Reality of God in our lives and all creatures great and small without fear.

What is Fear? It is Feeling envy anger revenge, from the root word Fear and the opposite Life of Valued Energy [love], that is not a feeling. Fear has many other negative words based on a persons EGO, or situation not on another person's valuable compassion and care. Christ takes us through the final stage of growth. The phase of freedom without disorder, Law is not abandoned but made subject to justice, to repair damage or make adequate compensation where appropriate, not with fear but with responsibility. When God as the Spirit of goodness comes to live within us, we are prepared to accept God's gift of freedom inside us to pass on to the world around us.

When combined with gentle strength, because there is nothing as strong as gentleness and nothing as gentle as real strength. When we use gentleness instead of anger we get a creative, valuable well balanced energy Matthew 11 "learn from me for I am gentle and humble of heart, and you will find rest Spirit and Truth" hourly, daily prayer develops our intimate relationship with God. He gave us the Lord's Prayer.

Our Father in Heaven,
Hallowed be your name
Your Kingdom come,
Your will be done on earth as it is in heaven.
Give us this day our daily bread
And forgive us our sins
As we forgive those who sin against us,
Lead us not into temptation
But deliver us from evil.

This prayer is to teach us an attitude or frame of mind, as verbal communication is a part of encouraging us to pursue God's guided path. This requires honesty, and total sincerity with our self and God in our words and actions. This also requires us listening to God which may come to us from other people. However to hear God we must become sensitive to the deepest levels of our Being and place His values at the centre of our lives. As well as prayer, there is Cosmic Spiritual awareness of God with Meditation for the purpose of developing insight and healing. When the Spirit of Truth comes, you will be guided.JN:16:12-15. So what must a Christian do "Follow me" Jesus said in JN.1: 43.

Paul tells us in Romans 5:5 "the love of God has been poured into our hearts through the Holy Spirit" and in John 14:18 "you will not be left orphaned without a mother or a home". This passage maybe why the Holy Spirit has been considered a feminine attribute. The Holy Spirit is our guardian and speaks in our favour against negative voices that judge and condemn us. The Holy Spirit dwells deeply within us and is the valuable energy we are born with and both our Soul and the Holy Spirit give and receive to create shared truth and joy." Created in the Image and Likeness of God". Genesis 1:27, 5:2. This is often called our DNA which marks us as creatures of God, meaning we are male and female, body mind and spirit and contain the Divine Spirit which we call the Holy Spirit. This is our true Identity dwelling in us and considered the Original Blessing. "Likeness" is different and is only a gradual process as God loves His/ Her Image in us according to the early Mystics 2 Corrinthians.3:18. However we have not been and still are not capable of loving God sufficiently or either ourselves and one another, because we have lost the core message of our true worthiness of God's gifts of Love and Freedom. The old Prophets of Israel said there would always be a remnant Isaiah 4:3 as repeated in Matthew 13:33 in the metaphor of the yeast and Levin raising the dough. There are a number of Metaphors Jesus uses. MARK16:1-8 The Risen Christ represents the True Self the transformed and enlightened Soul.

MATTHEW 27:57 to 28:20 The Resurrection a mixture of joy and awe. Blocking the tomb, the earthquake, the women understand Jesus and the men hesitate the message "go tell all the nations".

LUKE 24 contrasts the ghostly presence and physical eating, which shows how our presence to others is how we are known to God. Then joy at the Ascension.

ACTS 1:9-12 the empowering Spirit will go to the ends of the earth but to keep our feet on the ground.

JOHN 20 and 21 Mary Magdalene John and Peter are the new informed believers as Jesus tells them "do not cling to me" in the new form of His body, and his presence brings joy peace forgiveness and the Holy Spirit through touching wounds, a new fire and catching fish 153 in number to symbolize the known Nations at the time. Peter is told LOVE [life of valuable energy] means to be a servant and go where God leads him even where he would rather not go.

MARK 9:2-8 and MATTHEW 17:1-8 and LUKE 9:28-36.

These are the 3 Transfiguration images that several believe are misplaced Resurrection scenes helping the main disciples with a mountain top experience, that has been placed in the middle of Jesus life to encourage and give the leaders confidence to go back down the mountain into the world and not be afraid. The challenge is for us to live through our Puzzle of Eternal Life with the help of the Holy Spirit. We need to know our true self first to understand the Divine experience as it is clouded with "unknowing" as in Luke 9:32 'until they awoke and saw Jesus Glory".

Our unconscious mind is the largest part of our mind which we are mainly unaware and when we work hard on our self-assessment we will discover it contains riches of imagination. We need to discover our birthright the Holy Spirit and practice drawing from this deep well within us. There is nothing we can do or earn to get the Holy Spirit it is already given at our birth we call our Soul. God does not impose this on us we have to personally accept and draw on this Divine indwelling Spirit. Some people are ignorant of the gift while others neglect the gift and miss the joyful benefits through lack of choice. The Holy Spirit has to be awakened in each person, recognized and realized in Romans 11:6 and Ephesians 2:8-10 then receiving undeserved radical Grace. True Spirituality is a search for Divine Union, hope and union is how Jesus finds us and also how Jesus found disorder and imperfection in humans in times of chaos and inhumanity to each other causing fear and uncertainty in what we think we can control. Knowledge should be balanced by failure, all success balanced by suffering to process the questions about love, death, suffering, eternity and God. My own mistakes failure, sin and humiliation means the future is always a little scary filled with confusion, lack of control, paradoxes and mysteries in the Gospel of John 5: 31-44 [the John is the Baptist] Jesus said "human approval means nothing to me and why waste time looking for approval from others when you have been given approval from the one True God."

Chapter 11

LOVE AND AWARENESS

1 Corinthians 13 and 1John 4:7-21

L.O.V.E. Life of Valuable Energy

A definition of Love for me is "Life of Valuable Energy" as Love is not a feeling, it is a decision of our will and there are two sides to valued energy conditional and unconditional [love]. A very large percentage of young men give undeclared conditional energy and women mostly give unconditional energy. Women undervalue themselves by accepting conditional love. Men undervalue themselves by not giving unconditional love. Men undervalue themselves by having self-esteem [over valued confidence] this is not a feeling. Self-love [love your neighbour as yourself] is to understand and accept their valued energy and true maleness, well nurtured in their youth means there is nothing as strong as gentleness and nothing as gentle as real strength. When we put gentleness and strength together we get well balanced creative energy, not sub-conscious anger. Men, for their Life of Valued Energy [love] need to learn where their unconscious anger comes from and bring it into consciousness to accept and manage their anger. This valuable energy derives from the word Love and Freedom with self-discipline and the positive feelings we have come from this self-control kindness, compassion, gratitude, joy, and thankfulness. This is self-discipline translated into action and any caring relationship is a disciplined relationship and shared Spiritual growth. Compassion is a feeling of great depth, a feeling uncontrolled is no deeper than a disciplined feeling. Good feelings are important and a source of our energy they provide the creative balanced power to accomplish our actions. This is the work of self-discipline that respects our feelings and prevents them becoming out of control and end up confusing and abusive. Genuine compassion is precious and thus freedom and discipline are partners for a constructive loving relationship and life of joy in shared Spiritual growth. This includes the respect and the separate identity of the loved one. Failure to recognize this causes much mental illness and suffering. This is called Narcissism and it is far too common for people to do this to their children and not allowing their true identity to develop. This lack of empathy can cause children emotional illness to find trustworthy people, to develop their own feelings and Identity.

This Book is my Voice and to hopefully encourage you to use your voice that is Gentle and Strong not angry and demanding which breaks the Confidence and Creativity of young boys and girls. My reason for putting meaning to Acronyms [that are the words we use daily] is to help unpack their deeper meaning. You can do it for your self and find the meaning of the words for you. Loving who we are is coming to terms with our own sensitivities and become Aware of our responses to others.

Awareness

For me is a felt sense like focusing which is a balance of concentration [heart/head] and communication[gut] on a subject of immediate necessity. For example a tennis ball while playing a game, as the intense focus allows a periphery vision [side vision]of the court. This occurs when the heart head and gut are all aligned in perfect balance in a person for total accurate placement of the tennis ball .A.W.A.R.E. for me means: Awake With A Revelation Experience. What do I need to be Aware? This is where I am now Alone but not lonely. I do not have a need to cling to people, that is what being

Alone means. Give up dependency that has suffocated your life, be it abuse, drink, drugs, gambling or people, everything will go on as before, you will continue to be in the world, you will no longer be of the world. In your heart you will be free at last. No one has the power to make us happy or miserable we do it to our self with issues or various problems. Jesus said "the birds of the air have their nests, and the foxes their holes but you will have nowhere to rest your head in your journey through life." If we ever get to this state we will know what it means to have Vision that is clear and unclouded by fear. To come to understand our life of valuable energy [love and freedom] we need for people and things to lose their importance so we can become totally aware of our true identity. It will be a help if we turn to nature for a while and silently commune with birds, trees, flowers, animals, the sea, sky, clouds and stars. This is a Spiritual Exercise to become aware of things around us. So to speak "smell the roses" will help us make contact with Reality. This is a cure for loneliness, at first may feel unbearable because we are not accustomed to Aloneness. Then we will understand what freedom is, what love is, what happiness is, what reality is, what truth is and finally what and where God is.

We may well ask what is love? what is freedom? It is not the lack of Religion that the world is suffering it is the lack of valuing our true self and each other, the lack of awareness of our God gifted valuable energy and lack of awareness of understanding the blockages we put in the way of God freedom and happiness. Turn on the light of Awareness and the darkness will disappear. Love is not something we produce. Love is who we are, gifted at our birth, we do not produce the wind, rain, sun or stars we surrender and value these things. We have been gifted a Body Mind and Spirit of Love [life of valuable energy] we need to become aware of our mistakes, addictions and fears so we can gain some insights into self-discovery, self-understanding and self-care to value our self, our families, neighbours and our friends. The communities in which we live are governed by the conflicts and blockages that arise from our fears and desires. Living in community needs our awareness to forgive the mistakes we and other people make to live in the present moment with fresh attitudes and valuable energy. We can do almost anything we want to in life provided we do not take away the freedom of some one else. Some one wiser than me said "every child born has God in them our attempts to mould the child will turn God into a devil." We have to be a special kind of parent to every unique child. There is no violence in a child when no one is using violence on them.

Do you know where wars come from? They come from men/women projecting outside of them their conflicts and fears that are inside them. Usually older men inflict their fears on young men/women when sending them to war. The change in our technology has changed the way we are living which means we need an overhaul and change in how we operate our humanity. We urgently need to train and educate our children with resilience and gentle strength to understand how to have self-control of themselves and others against inner conflicts and fear that is when a child has no violence in them. Men and women with Authority can be tough and effective with no hatred in them, like a surgeon when operating or a great teacher like Jesus, why can't we see this. Our freedom with discipline and God's guidance should be our responsibility. It is important I recognize my feelings are in me and may not be in the other person. Jesus was often tough and effective without anger. I believe we can help young children with these helpful attributes.

Responsible freedom helps destroy inner conflict. The root of all evil is in all humans and our freedom is in our free choice to prevent evil in our self with our life of valuable energy [love]. As we begin to understand this we stop making demands on our self and commence nourishing our Soul. This involves our feelings and what we feel when in touch with nature or a job we love in relation to our feelings when winning an argument or we win a race. The last feelings are worldly and the first ones are called Soul feelings. Lots of people live Soulless lives because they live on praise and popularity or being the Boss. So to gain happiness we need to nourish our Soul. Because of the changes technology has made and for women slowly gaining recognition of skills and ability, our humanity needs to change. This means to raise our children so they don't get stuck in a Soulless life. To find a well balanced freedom with learning resilience and gentle strength with shared power for true happiness.

SELF-ESTEEM is pride or Ego which is acquired by their efforts to have power and not to share power. This means molding others [women and men] to their selfish needs and manipulating them when making decisions.

SELF-WORTH /[SELF-LOVE is to value the other [women and men] the same as we value our self. When we do not value our self how can we value other people we need to understand it is not about changing other people, it is about valuing people as they are, they may have to change themselves when required. Women under value themselves when pretending to be other than who they are, so knowing our true identity is important. When a man loves / values a woman he is valuing her as he values himself, it is not a feeling, they come later. That is what Jesus Christ came to teach all of us, when we accept our birthright, our Gift from God of LOVE [Life of Valuable Energy] in our SOUL with FREEDOM. This is HOW we nurture and teach our children their unconditional Life of Valued Energy. When we do not accept God's Gift we damage our SOUL. It is also called self-destruction. Another name is Hell.

FEELINGS are GLAD—SAD—BAD we can have these feelings at our birth. They are not LOVE as such, they are how we experience the Life of Valued Energy we have been Gifted. Which means God is not into feelings they are part of the MYSTERY of Humanity and all Creatures great and small. God has given all His Creation a FREE WILL to make our choices and decisions, with His help when we ask. This LOVE and FREEDOM is HOW we chose to use our Valued Energy in our Life. This can be a life of GLAD, SAD or BAD feelings. It depends on how we are nurtured, guided and taught from the Cradle. LOVE is the will and decision that our parents or guardians use to help us have glad, sad or bad feelings. This is given in the most vulnerable stage of our life as we absorb into our SOUL the expectations of our future life we are suddenly made aware of as we begin to grow up our BODY—MIND—SPIRIT.

The more we become aware of pain we get defensive and find ways to defend our self. The sooner we get in touch and learn to express our true identity can help our awareness and courage with honesty to heal painful feelings and prevent negative reactions. Not all defense mechanisms are negative and can help us develop our emotional skills and strengths with other people's boundaries and autonomy and to discover our own. If we are not meeting our children's needs we may be acting out our own unconscious pain. Sigmund Freud believed there were common unconscious issues we experience in varying degrees. The following are five defensive mechanisms:

1. The Rejection Wound.—I'm perfect, to compensate by trying to be perfect in everything. This means I need to feel safe. We need to learn that making mistakes is normal and necessary for learning and growing. These people are often successful and are capable loveable people.

2. The Abandonment Wound.—I can't support myself, and are emotionally needy, and need others to feel safe and O.K. In relationships they become demanding of attention and feel angry if they don't get it. They often push the other person away and collapse as they see themselves as a victim and feel deeply unloved. They need to deal with their unconscious issues of anger and love themselves and use their intelligence.

3. The Betrayal Wound.—I have to win, these people are very competitive, dominant and often control freaks, "it's my way or the highway" and are insensitive to other peoples feelings. They are often manipulative, seductive, charming and like to be admired. When younger felt shamed by a parent who built them up then criticized and squashed them emotionally. As a defense mechanism they try to control all people around them to feel safe. They need to learn to value themselves and let go of dominating and controlling everyone around them. They often make good leaders with their desire to win.

4. The Hatred Wound.—These people often seem vague, lose track of time are unreliable and disorganized. Vagueness is a defense when a child may have felt unwanted or fear or grief from the mother at birth the defense is to tune out, or through an extreme traumatic experience of physical or sexual abuse. This makes them feel sensitive and intuitive.

5. The Autonomy Wound.—These people feel very controlled or smothered by parents while growing up, even with love by a person who is overly concerned that the child feels they can hardly breathe. These children are not given free independent choices and decisions. They often find it hard to express their deep feelings and wishes openly, instead indirectly or the silent treatment. They need to be allowed to express their feelings without fear or control. They have a strong need for space, are sensitive to people encroaching on their boundaries and need to freely express themselves. This experience they suffer develops their compassion and capacity for love.

When personal change needs to occur, the process is a matter of searching for a method that is appropriate to the kind of change that is needed. A helpful vision is required that a person hopes to gain then put the method into practice. As stated previously do not allow fear to erode confidence as it paralyses decision making and confuses our identity.

This Book is my Voice about reality, my life experience listening, study, reading and learning How to find a way of happiness through tragedy, then neglect and lack of care by removing my valued energy with over powering control. By taking away confidence, courage, creativity, communication and commitment by damaging lies and cruel selfishness these are the sad and bad feelings which we can over come with the glad feelings of kindness, gentleness, joy and strength with forgiveness. This healing means effort, and work on the Puzzle [you and me] when we have not received the early compassion and training required for Love [Life of Valued Energy]. This possible unintentional or mismanaged upbringing can be resurrected in our teens or older when we "'seek knock and the door will be opened".

My father forced me to marry a man I had not had a conversation with and did not like the look of him. He wanted to marry a wealthy girl so he could live off my inheritance, he was a lazy wastrel. And this was only told to me 3 months after we were married. I had no money as my father had cancelled my nursing application, and my Grandmothers support was pushed aside by my father. After three children in three years and one miscarriage and ten years of sexual abuse I became very ill. My husband said to me "don't you respect me" and I said "I respect you as a human being not as my husband you do not respect me" he said "I thought I could change you" I did not answer [I thought by vicious sexual abuse] I believe it is better not to get caught up in a perpetrator's angry verbal games. He said you are my wife I will have sex when ever I want it. You will have kids until I get a son. I said nothing and a few days later left with God's help. I found a way to forgive, create, share, inspire with God's gentle strength I hope to achieve in my life, not there yet. For me an Acronym of the word GENTLE means Good Essential News Tender Living Energy. Then for the word STRENGTH means Spiritual Trust Requires Early New Growth Then Health.

I play Bridge and it teaches me "It is not only the cards I am dealt but how I value and play the hand". THIS IS TRUE OF LIFE:

When I have to cope with tough experiences of life, I try to use my Valuable Energy and thoughtful compassion to help others as well as myself. To stop violence to myself it is important to use gentle strength and point out to the perpetrator it is not acceptable. This is where our three Brains, HEART, HEAD and GUT brains have to be balanced [congruence]. This is vital for making good decisions. All of Creation have both Love and Evil, and God gives us humans the strength and power to overcome evil, they are the two root words from which we make our decisions between "good or evil" they are not feelings they are our Will.

L.O.V.E. these letters stand for "Life Of Valuable Energy" all our positive words stem from the root word "Love" --kindness, generosity, compassion, care, respect, thoughtfulness, joy, peace, thankfulness, patience, faithfulness, self-control and gentleness, these are some of the good feelings. We also have help from our Intuition a deep inner Knowing that goes beyond our conscious mental process and when we recognize it the stronger and more accurate it gets. These ideas and messages from our three brains are sometimes called "a sixth sense" which can come from feelings, dreams visions {a quiet inner voice} and is calm and not fearful. Some researchers make a distinction between a pure head inner voice [Ego] and a heart/gut inner based voice because they say a heart/ gut voice comes from a focus of compassion, peace and courage. The warning here is if we omit listening to the head brain, which we need to practice so we become aware of the difference between the ego based messages and the heart/gut messages. For an example in a state of anger or fear our brains definitely send us intuitions and messages and these will be very different in quality to those from a state of kindness, and balanced calmness. It is helpful to practice balanced breathing to bring our brains into a state of calm and not fearful. I have found building "intuition muscle" works the same way as normal muscle exercise through practice. Albert Einstein said "the Intuitive mind is a Sacred Gift and the rational mind [brain] is a Faithful Servant. We have created a society that honors the servant and has forgotten the Gift".

Self-awareness is similar to Intuition, and requires listening to all messages and responses from all three brains. What our Head thinks about the situation, what our Heart senses and our Gut feels about the situation. It is important to separate our thoughts, feelings, responses and reactions. It is recommended to be aware of self-deception and overcome it. Our Head brain is capable of confusion, so find an honest balance possibly in our sub-conscious as we can deceive ourselves by only focusing on one brain, the head without the heart/gut can be dangerous.

Life Of Valuable Energy.

This Book is my voice, my life of valuable energy called LOVE. My reason for putting meaning to the Acronyms we use every day is to encourage men and women who are struggling to find meaning and purpose in their lives and how misinformation can destroy Confidence to have the Courage to move forward. When we need or want something we do not have, we go to some one else to acquire what we need. Mostly we go to a shop where we hope to find what we need, and ask the price---what value do we put on it. If we think the value is good, reasonable or too high we buy it or leave the shop. We do the same with people we meet in life. We correctly or incorrectly value our self and value the people we meet. Some we may want or need to see again depending on the value we give him/her. Our other gift of Freedom of choice is how we treat the person or need the person in our life how we value them and make our choice, which also depends on how we value our self. When we do not know our true value or even over value our self we make our human errors, mistakes sometimes sadly EVIL which means Energy Violent In Life, this can be physical, mental, verbal or spiritual. When we run out of valuable energy we humans search for more in the atmosphere [we want to fly like a bird] or in the ground to find energy to keep us going, living, growing, creating more power to give us energy. This is what Love is, our God gifted energy which we wear out or abuse. As previously stated LOVE is not a feeling, it is a decision of our will, feelings change 3 or more times a day. Our decision can be for life as in marriage or being a parent, it may be a short period for the hour or day or need in our life and we will have different feelings about the decision depending on how we value the person or need. If you do not value my voice you will make your own free choice, [that is O.K.] that is your LIFE for me means Living In Faithful Eternity or if you do not believe in God means Living in Free Energy. My reasoning is because we are living between the ALPHA and the OMEGA [the Beginning and the End] as the Bible tells us we live between our Creation [birth] and our Revelation Life with God.

I believe when we die we all go to God. Jesus said in John 14 there are many rooms. When we do not listen to anyone or God before we get there, my understanding is God's job is to allocate a room and God may well send those who do not listen into the same room. God may say "you did not listen to the people I sent to you or me" and maybe you will say "no one listens to me now" and God may reply "we all have to value and listen first to others and then they will listen to us". Then when you really listen to some one in the room the dawn of awareness will shine and you will find your true Heaven, because listening is caring about others and contributes to great healing and brings peace. This means coming to terms with our own sensitivities and owning our responses to others, and remains a mystery as to which room we will be placed.

When we frequently use the word Love as a feeling it is not adequate and unhelpful with its translation from Greek as the Greek language divided Love into various categories with several words for love with a better indication of the meaning for example:

1. Agape a word most used in the New Testament embracing self-giving a decision of our will not feelings. My desire is for your sake not my sake.

2. Eros a physical sexual desire about pleasure and gratification. Eros says I desire you for my sake.

3. Philia was thought by the Greeks to be the highest form of human value and is an intimate relationship of body mind and spirit.

4. Storage was the word used for the care of parents for their children and reverse.

Love is an act of our Will and a decision which implies choice, and love is not effortless to the contrary love is full of effort which is why my acronym is Life of Valuable Energy, and in marriage means two people choose to put each other first. A cornerstone of emotional awareness is a sense of self-awareness, which is an ability to pull back and recognize what one is feeling—either anger, shame or sorrow before taking action. The self- awareness is crucial because it allows us to exercise more self-control. Our Love, Life of Valuable Energy is how we operate our feelings of kindness, compassion, loyalty, honesty, caring, of intimate touch and feeling of being wanted. Self-love is the true value of our self as a child of God [warts and all] when a child understands this even when they feel challenged or want to do something a different way from the way we want something done. This is the valued energy [love] we impart to our children with the feelings of kindness and compassion. This brings me again to the five love languages we should learn for our self and teach our children.

1. Words of Affirmation—in other words encouraging messages which means to "inspire" courage. To communicate kind words that gain confidence this requires energy and empathy to see the world from your spouse or child's perspective. Humble words that make requests not demands that is what makes us feel appreciated and forgiveness which is not a feeling, it is a commitment to developing relationships as we need to know each others desires.

2. Quality Time---giving some one our undivided attention and quality conversation which requires not only sympathetic listening also self-revelation. When speaking with children ask them to look at you and when listening to your spouse do not do something else at the same time. Do qualities activities that you both share and enjoy.

3. Receiving Gifts---as some church services for marriage say the rings they exchange "are outward and visible signs of an inward and spiritual grace" a bond that unites two hearts in a life of valuable energy. This is not meaningless rhetoric, symbols have a meaningful value. The Gift of our self being there when our spouse needs us, a physical presence in a time of crisis and do not expect the other to read our mind.

4. Acts of Service---is chiefly doing with a positive spirit what our spouse would like us to do, such as washing the dishes, walking the dog, removing the rubbish or even washing the

car. Beware acts of service are not done out of fear, guilt or resentment, such as manipulation by guilt "if you were a good spouse you would do this for me" or by fear "you will do this or you will be sorry" both are lack of love. Our actions are often influenced by how our parents treated each other, so our emotions, needs and desires are in our personality, so criticism and demands tend to drive wedges in relationships, this is where self-awareness is very helpful

5. Physical Touch--- Physical touch is communicating valuable energy. Babies that are held, hugged, kissed develop a healthy valuable emotional life. The person whose primary love language is physical touch finds the message will be far louder than the words "I love you" and shouts even louder to a child when given a tender hug. Love touches may be Explicit and need full attention as in sexual foreplay for intercourse. This may take more time to understand how to communicate to your spouse. Love touches may be Implicit which requires only a moment putting a hand on a shoulder.

These love languages help us learn how to make decisions without destroying unity, how to give constructive suggestions without being demanding and clearly our bodies are for touching and not for abuse. These love languages by Dr Gary Chapman are valuable tools for men and women to enjoy valuable relationships. When practiced in adult relationships make it easier to discover in our children, using awareness and understanding of the responses that children find makes them happy and content. This valuable encouragement helps children grow up knowing they are loved and their true value as men and women. This gives confidence, courage, creativity and commitment to live a meaningful and purpose filled life. I believe this has to start at the Cradle our Birth.

It is one thing to ask and hope for investment of money from our governments, both State and Federal to help with health and education. But governments are not voted in to teach us how to raise our children to a life of valuable energy and nurture them. All parents are responsible for how children grow up physically, mentally, emotionally and spiritually. If for various reasons we may have had unhelpful experiences in learning valuable life skills we need to take courage with confidence and make our own changes for a more creative and meaningful life. This relates to how we adults and young parents need to examine our unconditional love [life of valuable energy] of family, neighbours and our friends. Mother Teresa said "we cannot do great things, we can only do small things with great love." God's total commitment to Love [life of valuable energy] brings a total commitment to Freedom which means God gave up enforcement and control. God is clearly not a policeman. No other way for God to act because God is Love itself, that Life of Valuable Energy that He/Her has gifted us. 1John 4:8,16,18.

Chapter 12

FREEDOM AND RESPONSIBILITY.

John 14:15-17. 2 Corinthians 3:17 Galations5:13

F.R.E.E.D.O.M. Free Responsible Energy Enables Discipline Of Mind

The gift of Freedom comes with God's Blessing at our birth. It takes guidance and energy to understand we do not earn this gift we are to value ourselves as we accept this gift. It is how we use our gift with truth and integrity that counts. This means we are to free ourselves from self-importance and self-accomplishment to help us in all our relationships. This requires some valuable energy called Discipline to balance our actions for happy results. Freedom needs the order of discipline so that life may have balance and direction. It has been said "Freedom is not the right to do what we want, but the power to do what we ought". Today the Laws we make are for the benefit for all of us to live together in unity and harmony, with all cultures and creatures great and small. When we abuse, ignore or have denial about our Civil Laws for Society we are not using "God's free Spirit" with valued honesty.

It depends on how we listen, understand and honor God's messages through Jesus of wisdom and freedom for all Creation. Jesus' messages are so we can best serve God, ourselves, the

Community and the World with hope and faithful responsibility. Any unhelpful traits and habits have to be unlearned to improve aspects of life that are hurtful and damaging, some say are "too hard". The only weak part is "our desire". With a real desire it is not that difficult. When we do not use our gifted energy for good outcomes we suffer the consequences. When developed it takes time to change aspects of anger, selfishness and fear, which have developed in our childhood, into healthier emotions and attitudes. We all have to work with these character faults and recognize it is OK not to be perfect. Demands for perfection only create anxiety or worse Depression. It is our responsibility to bring our children up with good character attributes of value, confidence, courage, and creativity as these create good communication and commitment for our free choices. This is essential if our future generations are to have purpose and meaning in their lives and not just Fear to survive. This is the responsibility we have to change and manage our humanity as technology changes our lifestyles.

There is no meaning in life unless we have a purpose for learning, even when challenging. We have thrown the "baby out with the bathwater" of God's gift of Love [life of valuable energy] and true Freedom with our selfish, misguided thoughts and fear. We are teaching our children "WHAT to think instead of HOW to think". They need to learn how to get their own truth. Life is a school in which we all have lessons to learn. So our thinking and mind games need a necessary overhaul. I heard a similar message to this from a Scripture teacher over 60 years ago, "there is nothing as strong as gentleness and nothing as gentle as real strength". Gentleness is not a weakness it is a virtue of a real man. Far too many of our present fathers are training their sons to be fearful and angry, which speaks very loudly how they experienced their own up bringing. By being role models of aggressive control, not understanding and valuing shared control. If men understood that strength and good order comes through Gentleness their maleness would be more valuable to themselves, their children and society. Parents need to be aware that boys are not being taught:---

1. How to solve conflict without violence.

2. How to live without irrational fear.

3. How to love without angry conditions and to learn unconditional love.

Jealousy and Rejection

Of all the possible faults we humans can have jealousy is the most self-destructive. Why? Because they are feeling unworthy and not getting all the attention they want. This comes from their deep sub-conscious planted in their childhood and not corrected. It is irrational fear and a sin of omission [not a crime] of God's gift of love and freedom at their birth. We are all valuable and worthy and we should teach our children this important attribute from the cradle, through their young years to adulthood by hugs, affection and words of praise. With discipline we have a free choice but we cannot make other peoples choices for them. When we know our true self and value we should not be jealous of anyone, male or female. Otherwise this can be selfish suicide of the Soul. If we feed positive thoughts to our sub-conscious mind of freedom, peace and love consistently we can overcome any addictions. We can prove the truth of our own inner resources of mind over matter. Our resources of courage, strength and self-care are in us, thank God so use them. This can be achieved by developing good habits this makes life easier for our children and us, when we teach them while young. For example, like riding a bicycle or learning to swim and later driving a car. Good habits that are consistently taught become part of our sub-conscious and then an automatic habit.

Men and women are not the same [equal]. We think and act differently, and it is very OK not to be perfect. Jealousy comes from the root word Fear. So ask yourself why you are fearful, it is not a crime, it is a feeling and feelings are important. We are male and female humans and understand our own skills and abilities, our joys and sadness which are all part of life. I have said men and women are not equal. However I do believe we should have equity [justice] and respect like men in the work place with finance and business as well as in the home and other relationships. Some women will do the same job as a man and should have equity in all aspects. The women may approach it from a different angle or process and in some situations have a better outcome. There should be justice at all levels

I had to learn early in my life about rejection, having my free choice forced from me. I discovered many women one way or another experience rejection in their lives because men want complete control, shared control is not on most men's agenda unless taught from birth. So hand in hand with Theology I have experienced and studied a great deal of Psychology over the years. These two faculties are both entwined in the New Testament. I have been trying to understand why men treat women and families, even those they love [their desired choice] with many varied facets and degrees of control. The statistics have long been known that older men look for a young woman to look after them when they come close to depart their earthly life. I know Alex did that is why I kept him at home and stayed with him which was a great comfort to him. His last words to me were "you are the kindest person I have ever known". Most men do not want to die on their own as it is fearful for them, as they do not like losing control. I am a believer in "freedom of choice" with love [life of valued energy] from God as we are to make our own choices for life, with the help of the Holy Spirit if we ask and are believers of Christ's teachings, parables and metaphors. I believe Jesus is the best psychologist the world has ever known, as His teachings are entwined with the best psychology as a recipe for living a meaningful eternal life. This is what many educators are exploring and discovering. So many people are beginning to recognize that the truth of the New Testament is REALITY and reality is the final truth for all of us. I and many today who study these faculties believe Jesus was God. The writers of the New Testament called Him the "Son of God", I believe they could not accept or understand the concept that Jesus really was God He called Himself the "Son of man".

In 1 John. 4:18 Jesus came to tell us that God is a God who gives us Life of Valuable Energy and is not a Judgmental God. We humans do all the judging then blame God. Far too many people play the "Blame Game" and avoid responsibility. I believe in the Old Testament the word "judge" was used in a more negative sense of punishment. When the New Testament was written I believe the word "judgment" was used in a positive sense. The New Testament tells us that Jesus came to dispel the judgmental God idea, along with many other human made ideas and rules regarding slaves, women and children. Many humans do not believe or recognize their birthright of Love and Freedom [with discipline] given by God. Some misuse their freedom for evil instead of good. God does not punish us, we punish ourselves with poor attitudes, decisions, anger and fear, and cause our own diseases and our problems or some times forced on us by others.

We need to empower men and women:-boys and girls.

1. To say NO to violence.

2. To encourage them to trust their feelings [our Spirit].

3. To maintain transparency and confidence with each other.

4. To allow each other to be heard.

5. To understand how vulnerable our children are to our actions.

A wise man once said "every child has God in them---our attempts to mould them can turn God into a devil". When a child feels loved he / she is OK, the child begins to treat others the way he / she has been treated, by parents, guardians and teachers.

To learn to share in the Divine Freedom is a gradual experience with God's generosity. Matt.20:15. To change our ego to a transformed state, removing our anxiety and insecurity, our true self finds it scary. Human society has become divided on this level of identity and our Spiritual Being. Though our society has become more civilized and educated on many other levels, many people still strive for attention and recognition and miss the contemplative awareness, of the silence filled calm and peace of Divine Freedom. 1 John.4-8, 16 God's total commitment to Love [Life of Valuable Energy] which means God is totally committed to our Freedom and gave up forceful control. God is clearly not a policeman. Love is both who we are and who we are still becoming, as we are in God and gifted a life of valuable energy at our birth. God never uses threats but leads us with persuasion and respects our gifted freedom. Jesus demonstrates Love increases our Freedom. Paul in Gal.5:1 confirms Jesus teaching.

Then we can understand how God's breath literally breathes life and forgiveness into the air. JOHN.20: 22-23. This is because Life and Love seek the same thing and that Love has overcome fear and anxiety. 1Cor.13:13. How over the years my dogs and horses have given me more unconditional love than many human beings. All creatures great and small who breathe God's precious air in spite of our appalling treatment of them, teach us in nature their unconditional love. I believe there is a great need for awareness of learned Communication for our children while very young and the following may be helpful.

Communication with Congruence

We need to learn how to communicate with our multiple Brains, our Heart, Head and Gut and bring them into balanced alignment. To listen to our Heart as it is our guide and compassion and provides our energy and direction for our values, then our Head for creativity of ideas and understanding to discover possibilities, so the Gut can offer intelligent courage to act with motivation. To learn to communicate this needs a good breathing exercise to follow as the sequence heart-head-heart-gut and back to heart is a tried and experienced suggested sequence. The heart will change with controlled breathing for positive emotions, values and connection.

Then the head brain brings in creativity in a connected way back to the heart which moves to the gut for action with a final balance back to the heart for a positive result. No doubt this exercise requires practice to help us balance our decision making experience. Congruence means to bring into balance which becomes clear our Brains do not operate separately from each other as they are connected via nerve channels and move backwards and forwards. You will find ways to teach this as I did to your children.

Chapter 13

WISDOM AND DISCIPLINE FOR HAPPINESS

1Corinthians 2:6-7 Proverbs 2:6 Proverbs4 :5-7.

W.I.S.D.O.M. When I Secure Discipline Of Mind

Wisdom is mainly found in the Old Testament in Job and Proverbs, and often refers to common sense and sometimes trying to find the meaning of life in difficult situations. Wisdom comes not from gathering experience [that can help] but more from how we experience what life throws at us. Do we learn and grow from the experience or do we continue keeping on with the less helpful decisions. Learning and education of self-discovery enables us to develop Wisdom, to thrive rather than just survive. Wisdom needs to be practiced in the way we live life as previously mentioned requires the involvement of our three brains to be creative, compassionate and courageous, to make things better for others in our community, ourselves when we begin to co-operate with God. These insights are our identity from the head, heart and gut brains perspective of how we take wise action in the real world. This means to align them we need to master the art of listening to them then, communicate them to practical life decisions and actions. Ideas that are not practical to change are a waste of valuable time and effort. Thus relationships, communication and organization are all important life areas of self-awareness, self-control, courage and health and are important for decision making and action.

Time is all we have, it is time right now to make your purpose for living a meaningful purpose for learning. Learn to find your truth and you will seek and find. My days are happier when I give people a piece of my heart, rather than a piece of my mind .Time requires good discipline, when we do not have Time for our children we are not able to observe them, to become aware of their special needs, and they are all unique and different. If we are impatient or irritated we may impose the incorrect discipline without checking the problem, or take time to consider the most appropriate discipline. For me this is where "there is nothing as strong as gentleness and nothing as gentle as real strength" is the way to start to teach children how to solve problems without anger or violence, with gentle urging praise and thoughtful care. Parents will observe how they play or talk, or when they run away from problems rather than face them, blame some one else rather than own up to their mistake. When parents are listening and watching their children they can respond gently with adjustments of strength with little stories or hugs and kisses, or pats on the back for honest answers. Sometimes this can be a shared suffering with a child and the children are not blind to this. This helps children realize that suffering that is shared with Mum or Dad is not so bad and cope better. This is the beginning of self-discipline. This quality Time tells children they are valued by their parents. If only words of affection are used and no action, the children are not deceived or can become confused by hollow words. The feeling of being valuable is essential for mental health and self-discipline. It is a direct product of parental love and such conviction must be gained in childhood. All children fear abandonment which begins about 6 months, as soon as a child is able to perceive itself to be separate from its parents and realizing it is totally helpless and dependent at the mercy of its parents for all forms of survival. This is the Time to cement Happiness not fear in our children.

In Matthew.9:28-30 Jesus said because you have faith I will co-operate with your sub-conscious mind, in the conviction that prayer would be answered, and their sight was restored. I have paraphrased this as I believe Jesus is the best psychologist the world has ever seen or known and we have not totally understood the depth of the living conviction of prayer. First clearly stated in Mark 11:24 what Jesus said to Peter "I tell you whatever you ask for in prayer, believe you have received it and it will be yours" I believe the organ of healing is the sub-conscious and the process of healing is Faith, Suffering and Forgiveness.

Old age does not have an impact on our Spiritual quality or power. Patience, kindness, humility, goodwill, peace, harmony are all attributes and qualities that never grow old. If we continue to use these qualities we will remain free and young in Spirit. It is not Time but the fear of time that is a harmful aging effect on our minds and bodies. What this reality means, they are afraid of life. It has been said that age is not the end of life but the dawn of wisdom. This is the awareness of the wonderful Spiritual powers in our sub-conscious mind that can lead to a happy productive life. When we believe this our sub-conscious helps bring this to happen. This is a change to a life more Spiritual and Eternal with wonderful senses that transcends the limits of our physical senses. This is Eternal life we read in John 17:3 our mind and Spirit do not grow old our faith and convictions are not subject to decay. We are as strong as we think we are with our life of valuable energy. We have much to give from our age of experience to the younger generation who seek the desire and capacity to listen. I am enjoying the Life of Valuable Energy, I am happy, serene and gracefully finding a harvest of a free Spirit of faith, joy, peace, kindness, gentleness, patience and self-control, thanks to Paul in Galations 5:22-26.

Happiness can be found in the power of the mind. The Book of Proverbs gives the answer. The happy person is who trusts in the Lord. Happiness is a state of mind. In Mark 11:24 Jesus said "whatever you ask for in prayer, believe that you have received it, and it will be yours". We have been gifted the freedom to choose happiness. Many people do not see the key to happiness. The great things of life are simple, gracious and creative, "fill all your thoughts with these things". Philippians.4:8 Paul says we can think our way with Christ into a life of happiness. Then Divine order takes charge of life every day when this becomes a desire, a spiritual habit, a spiritual state of mind. This then becomes power of the sub-conscious mind with God's help. If fear is a thought in your mind, dig it up and plant faith, victory over all problems. To be a happy person means to practice the best in our self, by expressing more of God's love, truth and beauty, the Spiritual laws of the sub-conscious mind.

What does it mean to be emotionally mature? No one likes to be criticized or rejected. However we have the ability to choose how to respond or react when it happens. The mature choice is to refrain from reacting in a negative way. I have learnt not to be offended. I accept the person's criticism or rejection as I know not to get hooked into some one else anger as that can be dangerous. Also I know I am worth more and it is not my problem, but the problem of the accuser. We humans are creatures of meaning, so if appropriate ask for the meaning behind the verbal attack. Depending how serious the accusation, apologize and if you can walk away from the situation. Do not indulge in negative unkind depressing thoughts. It has been said "our life is what our thoughts make of it" The truth is happiness is a mental and spiritual state. The happiest people bring out the best in themselves with a quiet mind. God is the best in us when we express more truth, care and kindness. We can rise above defeat when we trust in our Lord, this is the Spiritual law of the sub-conscious mind. To give thanks for our Blessings and keeping a state of Prayer through daily life and happiness returns answered often in hindsight. The state of happiness is seen and expressed in our thoughts and feelings. Then "we treat others as we would like them to treat us".Matt.7:12. this has both an inner and an outer meaning. The inner meaning is the connection between our conscious and our sub-conscious mind. The outer meaning is how we think, feel and act toward other people, as we would like to be treated. This with Matt. 7:1-2 to pass no judgments so we hope not to be judged. This is the key to happy relationships, also less angry, bitter or frustrated causes to health or medical problems. This is emotional maturity so we do not allow other people to upset our thoughts to make us angry, to be reactive and have negative response to criticism. The mature choice is to refrain from reacting in a negative way. Do not let anyone deflect us from our inner sense of peace and good health. When we have Love we are valuing the life energy of the other person and understanding their good will and respect, then we are honoring the Divinity in the other person.

What we call the aging process is really a time of change. The Bible tells us God is Life, and that life is Spiritual and Eternal. We need never grow old for life as God cannot grow old. We cannot see life, however we know we are alive and are here to express it in all its beauty and glory and learn how to trust God for the difficult parts. If we cannot run or kick a football, play a fast game of tennis or swim as we once did, or our body has slowed down, we can become renewed to another vital dimension of life. We call this growing old gracefully, which can bring the dawn of awareness of wisdom, peace, joy, good will and happiness, these qualities never grow old or die. Our character, the quality of our mind, our faith and convictions do not decay. Retirement can be a new venture, a new path with much to give from our life experiences to the next generation. We can refresh our mind to new challenges which are stimulating and interesting. When we reach this second half of life [usually past 50 years] becomes the Time and means the contemplation of the Truths of God. The fruits of age are the harvest of the Spirit of love, peace, patience, kindness and gentleness as Paul tells us in Galations.5:22-23. Old age is not a tragic occurrence, but each stage of life is a progressive move to a life that is Spiritual and Eternal. John.17:3.

To be afraid of aging is to be afraid of life. Spiritual Wisdom is passed on from person to person. In our sub-conscious lies the power of Wisdom waiting for us to develop and express it. This is using the deep truths our conscious mind has put there of new ideas, discoveries even inventions. Though Wisdom is invisible it is a beneficial friend. John17:17-21. We would be wise to grow old gracefully it has its own peace, wisdom, goodwill, love joy and happiness and these qualities never grow old they are eternal. The aging process is really change and not the years but is the Dawn of Awareness that creates the Dawn of Wisdom.

The Dalai Lama said "a calm mind is key to happiness" and 3 key skills that support self-awareness and self-control are:

1. Calmness.
2. Forgiveness.
3. Mindfulness.

Calmness comes from both the heart and gut when we accept reality and allow waves of stress to pass over us when sadness or crisis occurs take a deep breath to direct balanced breathing, into our heart then to our head and back to heart then to settle our gut. This is a true help to letting go of any stress. Forgiveness is the most powerful thing we can do for our self. It heals and stimulates positive states of being for compassion, kindness and gentle strength that are key components to happiness. Physical and mental health benefit when we practice these key skills. It is true that people who are angry, bitter or feel unfairly treated suffer from a higher risk of heart disease and only hurt themselves. Forgiveness is not a feeling, like love, it is a decision of our will and psychological evidence shows it is an important daily activity for a happier and wiser life. Important to note, forgiveness has 3 levels of mental [head] emotional [heart] and gut [action] in order to fully let go of any hurt at a deep level and the injustice no longer has power or control over us.

Mindfulness, we all make mistakes and no one is perfect. Physics tells us when we use our air-conditioner we cause Entropy [disorder] in the world, this cooling of the air to make a room cool we are causing Entropy by the heat we are generating in operating the air-conditioner. This produces a bigger amount of disorder to our environment than the decrease of Entropy to cool our room. This ultimately means what we do cause more disorder in the Universe. Therefore we live in a wonderful but imperfect world. So blaming or shamming our self or others around us does not heal or help our situation. To let go of negative thoughts and actions of anger and fear gives us self-control in a calm forgiving state to make decisions with a free mind. Some people think forgiveness is a sign of weakness I have proven to myself it is a sign of strength. It takes courage, [find it in your sub-conscious] and strength of purpose to practice forgiveness for our healthy fulfilling life of valuable energy. We can choose positive feelings and thoughts and apply them to our heart, head and gut, through our practiced deep breathing. There is also good help available and do not hesitate to ask for it or search out what is available where you live. We are precious people and need to look out for our self as well as accept help from others. To help us understand how Time and Happiness are related as many humans have not been taught how to handle Law and Freedom at the same Time. This is vital for creative tension and we need to learn this as early as possible to prevent us from making judgments, and comparing things before understanding and learning from complex situations then, to take Time to achieve results with an inner freedom and peaceful attitude.

Chapter 14

GRACE DOUBT AND RESURRECTION

John 1:14 John 20:1-2 Luke 23-34.

.G.R.A.C.E. God's Reasons And Christ's Ethics
**Those who endeavour with faith and God's Grace to
complete the puzzle will realize God knew
human kind failings so He showed His power
by raising Jesus.**

God is life. What people call death is to a new dimension of life, this shows us God will raise us through our suffering and death to a new life. Nothing happens to us without it being sanctioned by God and then only if it is potentially conducive to his/her long term yearning for God's goodness. If this were not so, His love for us would be inconsistent and unreliable. Christ assured us that" not one sparrow falls to the ground without our heavenly Father first having given His consent, as for you, even the hairs on your head have been counted. So fear not, for you are worth more than many sparrows." The reasons also lie as much in our realm of responsibility as it does in God's responsibility for His creative order. This is called co-operation with God's creative order, as nothing happens to us without God knowing. He does not and cannot prevent us from using the freedom of choice He gave us at our birth, often to our own failings and tragedies. However even in the midst of those who are suffering, God in Christ is with us, strengthening and supporting us. That is what Easter is all about. God did not want Jesus killed.

On Easter Sunday each year, Christians celebrate the Resurrection of Christ, and the miracles that Jesus performed in raising others from the dead His evidence to us of existence of Eternal Life. On this hinges the faith of all Christians. In my life time we have had an increasing number of recorded near death experiences, where all known body and brain functions ceased and the people were later revived. Their account of their experience provided evidence that life does not end when visible signs have disappeared. These people have completely lost their fear of death as a result. There are arguments that they may not have died or may have suffered from hallucination. However for those who are willing to accept the evidence, I am, and follow Christ to the best of their abilities, the death of their physical bodies need not be anticipated with fear and finality, but welcomed as a transition to an even better and fuller life. Jesus showed us suffering is not the end, He returned home and so can we, as love and suffering are our greatest teachers if we allow it to be so.

Many people in the world have been turned away from God because of painful experiences. In our culture God gets blamed for just about everything. This is evident in our Insurance Policies where excluding payment for damages or injuries caused by Acts of God, such as floods, earthquakes, hurricanes, tornadoes and forest fires caused by lightning. These are the reality of nature and we have been given the mental capacity to avoid building in areas with risk of future flooding, and many opportunities not to live or build in dangerous and vulnerable places such as volcanoes and low ocean frontages. Also neglect to make sensible, reliable storages of water in the land. We waste our opportunities to work with God and nature. It does not help or heal us to blame God for the storms and the disasters of nature that hit us, when we place ourselves in vulnerable situations, which raises pain levels and self-pity which causes anger that if not corrected can imprison us. This can also become self- destructive when blaming other people when involved in arguments, personal or family accusations. I was sent to boarding school for the 10 years of my education and was very happy and well cared for the entire time. However I know of another girl who was still angry with her parents until she died, for sending her to boarding school. She ruined her own life by her anger and negative attitudes, when she could have found forgiveness and a peaceful life. If she had accepted that her own thoughts were keeping her in pain, and that forgiveness would bring her true freedom. We make our own choices, as that is the Freedom God gives us all at our birth. This does not mean we condone the behaviour of our parents or who else may have hurt or injured us. Even if they never know our forgiveness, we will find forgiveness heals our-self. This is important to realize because we often hide the anger we feel about others as well as about ourselves. That anger is what makes it so difficult to forgive. Our lack of forgiveness creates tension that limits our relationships and attacks our bodies with various diseases.

When some one close and dear to our heart dies, there can be a flood of emotions. The physical grief of losing such a person can be immense. Some people deny their feelings by not shedding tears. Others can cry for months or years. If some one dies after a long painful illness, family and friends may feel relieved. Your Ego, mainly male may make you feel guilty for not having such emotions. Even others feel angry at God. Some Doctors tell people they should stop crying and get on with life. We all need to know there is no prescription for how a person should mourn or face death. These people need unconditional care, compassion and acceptance. There is a Spiritual way of healing as our minds can communicate without a physical presence. This with practice can lead to forgiving the person for dying.

The world is waiting for us—why you may well ask? How? The Gospels have opened wide the doors to the whole world. Jesus has ascended, gone back to be God and sent His Holy Spirit to be in us. Now He invites us to be messengers of the Gospels, bringing His Hope and Love that He gifted to us at our Birth, and the people of every nation, culture and race, friends, families and neighbours. Today the world is truly at our doorstep. We live in an age where we can easily travel to the other side of the world as satellite communication has shrunk the world into a Global Village. More and more our own local communities are made up of a rich diversity of people from other nations and cultures, with so many exciting opportunities to preach the Good News and become involved. Jesus promises to be with us in our adventures of life, He gives supernatural power and strength to us as we take risks with Him for Him. One day every knee shall bow and every tongue confess that Jesus Christ is Lord.[Phil. 2:10-11] and the joyful truth is that we can be part of His plan in helping to make that come true. Ask the Lord to give you heart for the opportunities that come to you and consider ways you can be a changer. Even at our senior age opportunities to offer the Good News are really possible. How God uses ordinary people to do extraordinary things.

Please do not be one of those people who sing the wonderful Hymn, "Here I am Lord, then say, "send some one else Lord." It does not take a Rocket Scientist to see that all God's heroes were and are very ordinary people. The thing that makes the difference is that they have a relationship with an extraordinary God living within them. This is a privilege accorded to every one of us who recognizes and wants to know God. God is working on two fronts all the time, as He works to transform society, He is working to transform the transformers. God changed Moses, Aaron and Miriam as they were changing their world thousands of years ago which we read in Exodus, Deuteronomy, Leviticus and Numbers. The reason that Moses gives me so much hope is that he shows us his failings---just like mine---ordinary and inadequate, helps me grasp Moses sense of failure. All of us feel inadequate in some measure, whether it is a case of being over our heads at work or at the bottom of the class at University, or clumsy on the sports field or responsible for an aging and difficult relative. We can all think of a situation in which we come up short. Maybe divorced, single parent, confronted by a teacher about a discipline problem at school, you feel intimidated. Do we say, "Here I am Lord send some one else." There may not be anyone else to send. There are all sorts of reasons to feel inadequate, how do we decide what to do? This is called a "Moses moment", there are Moses moments of doubt for all of us.

The marriage of your son is coming unstuck, you never really got along with your daughter-in-law, and now your son asks you to speak with her. This is a Moses moment. We can feel inadequate a thousand times a day, about a thousand different things. Relief comes when first we realize we are indeed hopelessly inadequate then we realize we have God. We can't----He can. We are inadequate----God is not. Finding and knowing our Identity is a key to unlock our inadequacies. When we understand we belong to God we find an assurance which settles our heart. It maybe this issue has never been settled. We may know about God --- but we do not know Him, we have not accepted Jesus into our very Being—our Soul—His Peace. JN.14. Once we know we belong to God, that He is in control guiding us, we begin to feel adequate in the face of our problems. We may belong to our family, friends, club or business, but we need to belong to God first. He made us---He died for us----we are twice His. A man I was talking to not long ago told me 'I have left the church" I replied, " you can't , church is not some where you go, church is who you are, you can't leave who you are". We are members of the Body of Christ. When we finally understand Jesus in John's Gospel telling us "He is in the Father and the Father is in Him" that tells me Jesus is God, then we are to follow Jesus commitment that "Jesus is in us and we are in Him". Jesus sends us His Holy Spirit to guide us, to strengthen and give us His healing salvation. Then we will listen to His Wisdom and Power to lead and teach and be messengers of His Good News for living an abundant life in our homes, our communities and the world. I suggest reading the Gospel of John aloud to yourself you will hear the very clear message many people do.

The following are a few clues from the many stories and parables in the New Testament that may help you find a few pieces missing from your puzzle.

1. God takes the initiative in healing man.

2. Jesus who died on the Cross was God become man.

3. Jesus the Christ fully identified himself with mankind

4. Christ died for us, and somehow retained sin in Him, a Mystery.

5. The cross was a process satisfactory to God to teach us His Power.

6. Jesus transferred us from being slaves to rebellion against God to being God's free children.

7. Jesus' death was not the end of Life He is alive now and lives within us as the Holy Spirit for God's purposes.

My understanding of death:

Our Body---Brain---Will is our earthly state. At our final earthly life our body, brain and will are discarded.

The Body---Mind---Spirit we are born with and in our final death our Mind and Spirit go with us to God as our Body is transformed to a Spiritual Body.

Like God's air that we breathe and the wind we cannot see but we know as part of our experience. The Spirit we cannot see but we can experience its presence. Those who endeavour with Faith and God's Grace to complete their Puzzle will realize God knows the failings of human kind, so He showed His Power by Raising Jesus. People ask what happens to our Soul when we die. My understanding is our Soul is in Eternal communion with God through the Spirit within us. This depends how the Spirit is revealed in a person's life and experience heaven and hell in their life. As previously stated I do not believe we are sent to hell after we die. However through our judging and blaming we do suffer and we can and do experience hell on earth. Because evil is in our psyche which can appear as a destructive power in all creative relationships and productive growth. In our world of good and evil these work in opposition in our conscious and sub-conscious and beyond our understanding, which Paul explains in 1 Cor.15:52 to show how there is a balance in Creation how growth, decay, death and re-birth are the forces in combat till the end of Time.

The Souls of humans cry out against these sufferings. However when we hear Jesus we understand the ultimate reality of Creation is Divine. This requires accepting the life of powers of Love and Evil in our lives and to love God as God first loved us 1John 4:19. Our suffering, the pain of loss and the inner pain of self-discovery is the means by which we are fully open to God's Love. This brings to our attention how lonely we are by nature, as with true suffering our gathered friends disappear. Jesus experienced this after the betrayal as His disciples fled in horror and amazement and Peter denied Him on three occasions of ever knowing Him. This unreliability of friends and family is from embarrassment and security which is challenged. It is possible to feel alone even in a large crowd. There is a paradox of human relationships where we use companionship of other people to avoid true communication with the other person, because true communication requires giving full attention of oneself to another person. This is the Spirit of Fear which uses anger, hatred or jealousy to remove any connection for plans or ambitions. Anger becomes dangerous and destructive when unreasonable. This suffering is often called the Hell within and is part of our psyche. This will cause our inner security to be challenged with outer possessions of money, prosperity, social position, mental intelligence or bodily health, before we become needful of Salvation. Until as individuals we find the core of reality, the centre of our Soul and discover the flaws in our own personality. This being our love, faith and trust in God, which is planted in our Soul where the Holy Spirit joins us eternally to God.

Resurrection

There are many ways we experience Resurrection during our life. For example;

1. To apologize when we hurt someone else.

2. Seek to change myself before trying to change other people.

3. Choose to serve others rather than to be served.

133

4. Give attention to those in pain or disabled.

5. Seek justice and the common good.

6. Do not identify with fearful negative, judging and blaming thoughts.

7. Remember God's gifts of Love and Freedom bring God's promise the Holy Spirit's Eternal guidance. John 14:25-27

Resurrection tells us there is a gate or door we must pass through and die to our false –self before our final death and this teaches us how to die and not be in fear or afraid of dying. Jesus showed us suffering is not the end. He returned home and invites us to return to our Spiritual home John 20:1-31 for us humans to hold in tension the whole Mystery of Life, we need to balance it with our Doubt, Death and Resurrection. Some pieces of our puzzle may elude us. However I like Albert Einstein's Wisdom "whatever Reality is it will show itself as simple and beautiful". I believe that is God's intention and hope for His Creation. Deut.6:4-7 long ago was the Creed of the Jewish people so they would not forget it. However Wisdom supports Mystery, doubt and unknowing, as our faith and value of God knows we are not God, and experiencing doubt we can ask and receive forgiveness. We are to remember that our life of valuable energy and suffering are our greatest teachers when we allow them to be. Phil 2:11-13. God's total commitment to Love becomes a total commitment to Freedom, which means God is not a policeman and gave up imposed control to humanity.

This leads me to Grace considered to be a force other than our conscious will. The reality of Grace remains unexplainable within our understanding of science and "natural law" and is considered miraculous and amazing. It is a force the mechanics of which humans cannot yet fully understand. For me Grace is the gentle nurturing female nature of God which is in balance with the gentle strength, care and protection of the male nature of God. I believe Theology is now blending Science with the wonders of God's Creation. For an Acronym of GRACE for me means God's Reasons And Christ's Ethics. The Greek Religious usage means

"Divine Gift" or "Favour". The English word "graceful" reflects this meaning. The foundation of the New Testament meaning of Grace is given in the Hebrew word "hesed" depicting God's Mercy and Love through which He overcomes and redeems the sin of his people. This expresses the loving action of God in Jesus Christ and means the Divine forgiveness and power of God communicated to those people who enter the new life of faith, hope and love. Thus Paul says in Romans 3: 24.we are justified by His Grace as a Gift. The central meaning always remains the mercy and forgiveness of God given freely to sinners. The power of Grace always remains God's Power but can work through men and women and fulfills, sustains and renews human nature. This is how Grace is understood in Christian Tradition to live a moral life which includes responsible human freedom and this Grace is called the Spirit of forgiving love, the life of valuable energy. Divine compassion and mercy in one direction and a more creative Life of Valuable Energy that is stronger than death. Love is conscious but Grace is not and Spiritual growth is the evolution of an individual. Spiritual competence may increase until the moment of death however life offers us limited opportunities for spiritual growth and the meaning of Grace, and be aware to take up the opportunities when you get them.

Grace is who God is and Grace is everywhere.

APPENDIX

I am living between the ALPHA and OMEGA the Beginning—my birth and the End—with God. This Book is my values, my voice and persuasion with Love and Trust in God, for Living in Faithful Eternity with a Life of Valuable Energy.

Seek and the door will be opened. Have you been seeking your own Mystery Puzzle, who, what, when, where, why and how to find the pieces to your own puzzle. I have been seeking and searching how and why we can declare God a Mystery. From information in the Bible and extensive theologians experience of Creation and in all aspects of my life of reading, study, listening and learning plus my experience related in my four books. I have found God is a Mystery, and the Mystery is how and why God is with us and in us and even though God showed Himself in Jesus and has gifted us to be Co-creators with Him. We can feel and know His presence even though we cannot yet see Him. I have found that we humans are the Puzzle. It is our lives as individuals, as the Body of Christ, and the different cultural communities of humans in the Universe in which we all live. You may well ask "why are we the puzzle"? Basically we want to control God and each other to show Him by only using our own resources to gain self-esteem, to deny or reject God's goodness and guidance offered to us. So then pain and suffering become our Eternal experience not peace and happiness. Then the healing process can only come through suffering and Forgiveness through God.

Humans make their own Hell of problems and diseases. Hell is not a place we are sent to by God. The Puzzle is how do we find a good, healthy, happy existence with confidence, courage, creative communication and commitment in life? Where is this Puzzle? It is found in the pieces of human nature and behaviour of Body, Mind and Spirit, in our Conscious and Sub-Conscious values attitudes, thoughts and feelings. Finding the pieces and putting the puzzle together is a lifetime occupation, which involves Love [life of valuable energy]. God's gift at our birth with freedom, and energy, emotion [is energy in motion] requires Effort with committed communication. Each living Soul's basic aim needs to avoid irrational fear and accept the Imitation of God's true love in Jesus. If this is shown to us in our childhood we have a better start to developing a life of valuable energy and a creative well balanced power for a shared life with good communication and commitment. If we have not received this while growing up, now is the time to treat your self to God's mercy and wonderful compassion.

What we have to forgive in others may be something in ourselves that we have hidden from our own awareness and self-assessment and need to discover. God has gifted us with love and freedom [God does not make our choices for us] I am not telling people how to live, it is each and every one's Freedom of choice. It is our true self-discovery and self-assessment that will truly help us have more peaceful relationships, when we stop telling others how to live and start practicing love [their value] and forgiveness. The most powerful healer of all is forgiveness, is to ask God's forgiveness and offer it to others. To be happy all I have to do is give up my judgment of others, which is the quickest way to undo suffering and pain. There is nothing as strong as gentleness and nothing as gentle as real strength. Gentleness is the ability to treat people well, this is not a weakness. Creative energy is when strength and gentleness and our 3 Brains [heart, head and gut] are aligned and balanced. Then the toughness and tenderness of God which is in perfect balance wants the same for us. I hope and pray you have found a few pieces that are helpful to you, that you can pass on to others in kind and word. May our God of compassion and mercy lead us to His/Her Kingdom.

My Hope and Prayer in my final Message to Mothers and young women, when you are ready for you to seek and find a father to your sons and daughters a creative male of gentle strength, [is not weak] who will raise his sons with gentle strength NOT fearful angry strength from the cradle. Your daughters will benefit as well as you to avoid Domestic Violence. Mothers are precious, valuable bearers and sharers of God's gifted Creation to be helpers to encourage the Fathers of sons to teach and train true male Love [Life of Valuable Energy] and Freedom [For Responsible Energy Enables Discipline of Mind] to grow to be gentle strong disciplined male Co-Creators with God. This becomes a Shared Responsibility not an absentee Father. I know Mothers give great compassion and kindness to their sons, however the boys have been missing out from a true loving male connection, values and gifts while young [up to 20 years of age]. We females cannot teach young males their maleness to grow up understanding the difference between males and females and how to value the difference they need a well balanced Father or male guardian.

I believe we females have to learn we are not equal –the same as males, we think and approach things differently, even the same job may be approached from another angle and be a more effective result. We females need EQUITY, JUSTICE in the treatment of valued skills, knowledge and experience in our Shared World. My message to the Fathers with wonderful male values can give and bring to life our human puzzle. I persuade Fathers to start at the Cradle to raise the first 20 years of your sons to understand How Gentle Strength is the most effective, confident creative courage of the Human Puzzle, from the Cradle through the young years to a confident compassionate self-assessment in their teenage years to begin the School of Life.

My Acronym for L.I.F.E for me means LIVING IN FAITHFUL ETERNITY.

If you do not believe in God the meaning could be Living In Free Energy hopefully with discipline.

Life is the love the valuable energy we have been gifted at our birth to find how we locate food and water and our other needs. We look for it in the earth and atmosphere, to find clean air and healthy processes to move and develop a creative way of living for meaning and purpose through listening and learning. To use our valuable energy to seek, find and have vision for communicating values, of gentleness, kindness, truth, compassion, justice, and to be consistent. Then faithful energy will care for the human race, nature, all creatures great and small and our planet of Gods creative wonders.

Christmas is a time of giving gifts, most of us like receiving gifts. Watch how children enjoy life when opening gifts with love. Many of us humans do not yet understand that LOVE, Life of Valuable Energy is God's greatest gift we will ever receive. Love is not a feeling that changes three or more times a day. Love is God's Gift of Life, as Jesus was God's Gift to us in human form to show us how to live a meaningful, purpose filled happy life, and we murdered Him. WHY? I believe Good and Evil are part of human nature, and God gave us free choice of how we want to value God's Gift of Life and all our choices. When we ignore this gift we devalue it and sadly abuse life or either abuse our own gift or some one else abuses our life, and we have to ask God's help to rescue our gift with confidence to find our true self again. When we say "I love you" we are saying "I value your life" so much I want to care and enrich it with joy together. Then the problems [darkness] fade away and the Value of Life [the light shines] I pray you have found some pieces to add to your Life Puzzle. May you find Gentle Strength to give to others and for your self in a life that is well balanced and creative and may our God of Compassion and Mercy lead us to His Kingdom and the Grace of our Lord Jesus Christ the love of God and the Power of the Holy Spirit be with us now and ever more. My final Acronyms are:

M.Y.S.T.E.R.Y. for me means, My Yearning Spirit Trusts Every Revelation Yearly.

P.U.Z.Z.L.E. for me means, Preparation Under Zealous Zeal Living Experience.

PROVERBS. 3:5-6

Trust in the Lord with all your heart and lean not on your own understanding in all your ways. Acknowledge Him and He will make your paths straight.

MICAH. 6:8.

"He has showed you, O man/woman what is good, and what does the Lord require of you? To act justly, to love mercy and to walk humbly with God."

THE ALPHA AND OMEGA
The Beginning and End of Eternal Life.
Blessings from Reverend Pam Halbert.

REFERENCES

The Following are the List of Inspirational Authors I have been Reading over 60 years. Books-Tapes-Articles-Lectures I have named the author when I have used an exact quote from an Article or Book as I have searched to seek and share a deeper understanding of God in Jesus Christ the greatest psychologist who ever lived with the guidance of His/Her Holy Spirit, as well as study reference to six Bibles, The New International Version and Christian Growth Study Bible the New Oxford Annotated, The New King James Version, The Jerusalem Bible and The Message.

1. Archbishop Peter Carnley
2. Archbishop Huddleston
3. Thomas Merton
4. Meister Eckart
5. Matthew Fox
6. Desmond Tutu
7. C.S.Lewis
8. M. Scott Peck M.D.
9. Anthony de Melo

10. John Eldridge

11. Richard Rohr

12. Paul Tillich

13. Clayton C. Barbeau

14. Alastair Campbell

15. Kubla – Ross

16. Carl Jung

17. Martin Israel

18. Angus Cullman

19. Grant Soosalu

20. Marvin Oka

21. Carmel O'Brian

22. Billy Graham

23. Joseph Murphy PHD.D.D.

24. Gerald G.Jampolsky M.D.

25. Neale Donald Walsch

26. Maggie Dent

27. Albert Einstein

28. Alan Richardson.

OTHER TITLES

DESERT DEACON (2015)

A GIFT OF GRACE (2016)

FREEDOM REVISITED (2018)